Physical Characteristics of the Welsh Terrier

(from the American Kenne

Topline: Level.

Loin: Strong and moderately short.

Body: Shows good substance and is well ribbed up.

Tail: Docked to a length approximately level (on an imaginary line) with the occiput.

Hindquarters: Strong and muscular with well-developed second thighs and the stifles well bent. The hocks are moderately straight, parallel and short from joint to ground.

Color: The jacket is black, spreading up onto the neck, down onto the tail and into the upper thighs. The tan is a deep reddish color.

Height: Males are about 15 inches at the withers, with an acceptable range between 15 and 15.5. Bitches may be proportionally smaller.

Weight: Twenty pounds is considered an average weight.

Feet: Small, round, and catlike.

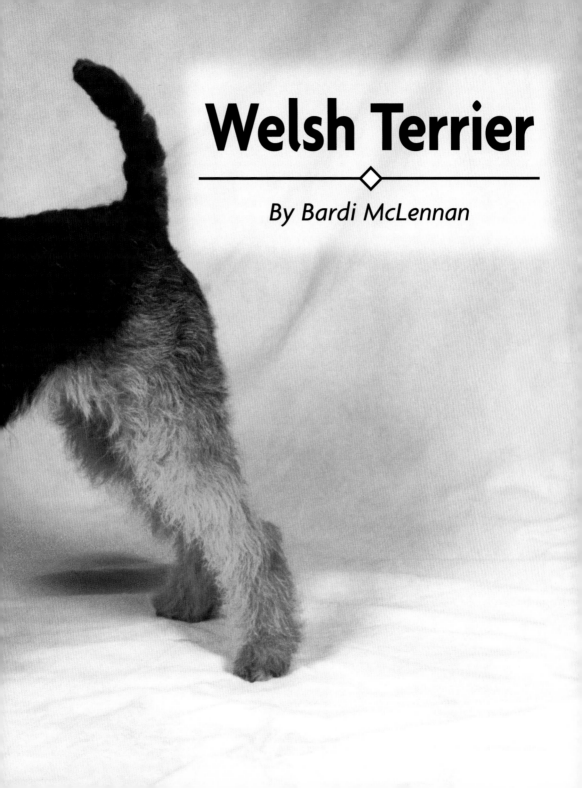

Welsh Terrier

◇

By Bardi McLennan

Contents

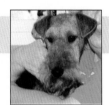

KENNEL CLUB BOOKS: **WELSH TERRIER**
ISBN: 1-59378-294-2

Copyright © 2005 • Kennel Club Books, LLC
308 Main St., Allenhurst, New Jersey 07711 USA
Cover Design Patented: US 6,435,559 B2 • Printed in South Korea

Photography by Carol Ann Johnson and Michael Trafford with additional photographs by:

Ashbey Photography, Paulette Braun, Linda Brisbin, T.J. Calhoun, Alan and Sandy Carey, Carolina Biological Supply, Isabelle Français, Chris Halvorson, Carol Ann Johnson, Bill Jonas, Dr. Dennis Kunkel, Bardi McLennan, Melia Photography, Tam C. Nguyen, Phototake, Jean Claude Revy, Hiroshi Saito, Chuck Tatham "The Standard Image" and Top Dog Photos.

Illustrations by Patricia Peters.

The publisher wishes to thank all of the owners whose dogs are featured in this book, including Ms. Wendy Allen, Judy Averis, Mereda Cornick, Gillian Griffiths, Mrs. M. Kelles, Mr. Juha Korhonen, Sari Mäkelä, Anne Maughan, Cathleen Saito, Dave Scawthorn, Kim Skillman and Linda Taranto.

Glansevin Coquette and Eng. Ch. Glansevin Coda, in a painting from 1907, illustrate quality Welsh Terrier type of that time.

WELSH TERRIER

THE WELSH TERRIER ORIGINAL

There are no written pedigrees before the 1800s for the small black and tan terriers bred by Celtic farmers, but clear references to them, including their monetary value (three curt pence), can be found in writings from as early as the 10th century. The dogs, like their owners, worked in the soil, hence the name "terrier," taken from the Latin *terra,* meaning "earth." These small dogs helped rid the farms of all forms of vermin from mice to martens and provided an occasional rabbit for the dinner table. They were true workers, and when their job was done they had earned the right to relax by the fire with the family. Thus a sensible temperament has always been intrinsic to the breed: sensible and single-minded working in the fields or alone underground; agreeable working with other dogs; steady and reliable in the home.

When it was found that fox hunting benefited from the addition of terriers to the packs of hounds in order to bolt the fox, the terriers' worth was raised a notch. However, it was due to the rapid expansion of dog shows that the Welsh Terrier gained popularity and prestige in the Terrier Group and became the handsome dog we know today. An opposing view holds that dog shows have put the cart before the horse by placing the emphasis on conformation and looks rather than on intelligence and working ability. Fortunately, this is not true in all countries.

In the beginning, the Welsh Terrier was little known outside his Welsh environs, which, at one time, went far beyond the boundaries of Wales as we know it today, encompassing a portion of the Continent and stretching into present-day Scotland and England. It is based on this historical fact that many in the breed feel so strongly that the breed eventually named the Welsh Terrier was indeed the progenitor of the other black and tan terriers inhabiting the British Isles.

Around 1450, a Welsh thank-you note (*Englyn diolgarwch*) was written, acknowledging the gift of a terrier. It reads in part, "And a

Welsh Terriers from the renowned Brynhir Kennels of leading breed advocate Walter Glynn in the early 1900s.

good black and red terrier bitch to choke the brown polecat and to tear up the red fox." It is quite possibly the earliest written description of the Welsh Terrier— a dog that was black and tan (the same "red" as a fox) and a worker of note.

The breed was known to have been used with the Glansevin Welsh Hounds from the early 1600s, and records of 1760 show that these terriers had also been used for several generations by the Jones family with their Ynysfor Otterhounds.

WHAT'S IN A NAME?
In the first dog shows where Welsh Terriers were exhibited, the classes were all-inclusive; for example, "Working Terriers" or "Any Variety Terriers." The individual naming of each breed occurred with the

increase in dog shows and the establishment of The Kennel Club of England in 1873. In the case of the Welsh Terrier, The Kennel Club was to become the arena for conflicting national canine contentions to do battle!

The Welsh people had always considered the black and tans as their very own, referred to as *daeargi*, of course, not as Welsh Terriers. The English now laid claim to their version of the black and tan terrier as the taproot of the breed under several elongated names such as the Old English Broken-Haired Black and Tan Terrier or the Old English Wire-Haired Black and Tan Terrier. So it was that in 1885 The Kennel Club had an international crisis of sorts on its hands.

A decisive event had taken place a year before in Pwllheli, North Wales: the first show with separate classes for Welsh Terriers, a specialty, if you will. On August 28, 1884, at the Lleyn & Eifionydd Agricultural Show, two highly regarded elderly Welshmen, who had bred these terriers for many years, were asked to judge an entry of 90 dogs, divided into three classes. Mr. Griffith Owen and Mr. Humphrey Griffith spent the entire day going over the dogs one at a time, each dog being judged on its own merits, not compared to any other dog. It is said that all were pleased with the results, which today in itself might

CANIS LUPUS

"Grandma, what big teeth you have!" The gray wolf, a familiar figure in fairy tales and legends, has had its reputation tarnished and its population pummeled over the centuries. Yet it is the descendants of this much-feared creature to which we open our homes and hearts. Our beloved dog, *Canis domesticus*, derives directly from the gray wolf, a highly social canine that lives in elaborately structured packs. In the wild, the gray wolf can range from 60 to 175 pounds, standing between 25 and 40 inches in height.

be considered something of a miracle!

ACTION!

In these early years, Welsh Terriers were most numerous in North Wales, and it was said that Cledwyn Owen, William Jones and Price O. Pughe knew all the Welsh Terriers in the area as well as their pedigrees. By 1885, Welsh terriermen (including Owen, Jones and Pughe) had had enough of the name nonsense and, with nine others, formed the Welsh Terrier Club. They were recognized by The Kennel Club in 1886, whereupon, in what can only be

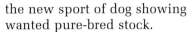

described as an act of diplomacy, The Kennel Club provided classes for both the Welsh Terriers and the Old English Broken-Haired Black and Tan Terriers (OEBHBTT). However, that was not to be the end of the story. Things began to fall apart for the Old English supporters, who never were able to put together an organization to back them. Nor did their dogs help matters.

For two years, 1885 and 1886, no OEBHBTT shown was from the mating of an OEBHBTT sire and dam. All were first-generation cross-breds. The dogs were said, in general, to be some-what more handsome than the Welsh Terrier, but since they were manufactured and could not reproduce in kind, this alone would seem to give credibility to the Welsh Terrier as the true black and tan. It should be noted that in those days there was no Kennel Club ruling against cross-breeding, but serious breeders in

the new sport of dog showing wanted pure-bred stock.

The results during those two years bordered on breed chaos, for many dogs were shown—and declared winners—in both classes. For example, one dog named Crib was shown as an OEBHBTT, but had been sired by a well-known Smooth Fox Terrier out of a solid black rough-coated bitch. He was also known to be deaf, a fault that the judges of the day apparently chose to overlook.

A dog named Dick Turpin was also famous for being caught in the middle of the dispute. The dog was Welsh-bred, but changed owners four times. Each owner was apparently unsure where to enter the dog, so Dick was entered in both OEBHBTT and Welsh Terrier classes. The show results proved his heritage, because he won a first place only when shown as a Welsh Terrier.

AND THE WINNER IS...

The Kennel Club ended the battle, and on April 5, 1887 dropped the Old English, etc., leaving the Welsh Terrier as the only recognized breed. One has to wonder if the long, clumsy OEBHBTT name may have influenced The Kennel Club's decision.

It should be noted that the Welsh Terriers entered in these early shows were, for the most part, a far cry from the beautiful dogs we see in the ring today.

STAND BACK, PATAGONIA!

It is now fashionable, especially among the young, to speak Welsh in Patagonia, an area of Argentina originally settled by the Welsh in the 1800s. Teachers have been sent there by the Welsh Office in Britain with an added plum for the students—six annual scholarships to study Welsh in Wales.

They were still primarily working terriers and meant to look the part. Cropped ears, for example, were allowed, since terriers' ears were often ripped by prey. The breed was not yet consistent in size or type. Many dogs had unattractive broad heads, drooping ears and white feet. The looks of the scruffy working terrier improved when popular opinion demanded it. The fashionable Wire Fox Terrier was what the public admired, and no doubt crosses with the Welsh were made to the Wire Fox. Judging from existing photographs, quite a few of these early dogs would be considered satisfactory breed specimens today.

EARLY SHOW DOGS
At the Bangor show in 1887, a bitch appropriately named Bangor Dau Lliw (Bangor Two Colors) became the first Welsh Terrier bitch champion. She was bred and owned by Mr. Dew. At this same show Walter Glynn, who was to become the leading advocate of the breed, exhibited his first Welsh Terrier, a male puppy named Dim Saesonaeg (No English). Bred by Mr. Pughe, the dog was made up a champion in 1889. He was highly regarded in his day. However, his son Eng. Ch. Cymro-o-Gymru (The Welshman from Wales) became the leading light of the breed. Bred by J. Mitchell out of

---

WELSH ROOTS AT BULLDOG UNIVERSITY
Elihu Yale, founder of Yale University in New Haven, Connecticut, had close ties to Wales. His family was from Plas-yn-Ial and although Elihu was born in America (where the spelling of the family name was changed from Ial to Yale), he retained his Welsh roots to the end and is buried in St. Giles Churchyard in Wrexham, Wales. As an acknowledgment of this association, a replica of the St. Giles tower stands at the university.

Mitchell's bitch Blink Bonny in 1891, Cymro won 27 Challenge Certificates (awards at Kennel Club shows) and for many years was thought to be the embodiment of something close to perfection in the breed.

The first dog champion was made up in 1887. Mawddwy Nonsuch, sired by Fernyhurst Crab, was said to be a dog with an excellent head, albeit with

Eng. Ch. Bangor Dau Lliw was a record-breaking champion in the 1880s. In 1887, she became the first Welsh Terrier bitch champion.

Eng. Ch. Vaynor Again, a male Welsh Terrier born in 1928.

cropped ears. Nonsuch was purchased by Edmund Buckley (Master of Otterhounds in Merioneth) for what was, at the time, the huge sum of 200 guineas. Possibly due in part to this extravagant expenditure, or the fact that the dog was said to lack type, doubts spread regarding the authenticity of the dog's dam. The gossip may well have been true, since apparently he was never used at stud. Eng. Ch. Bob Bethesda, a dog of Buckley's own

Eng. Ch. What's Wanted caused a sensation when she appeared on the show scene as a puppy during the 1919–1920 season. Her debut was followed by a brilliant show career.

breeding, was made up a champion soon after and was highly acclaimed as a show dog and for his excellent temperament.

The breed was gaining much attention throughout Wales, as well it might, for this was also a period of intense Welsh national pride. As the number of dog shows increased and the dogs proved themselves winners in competition, the popularity of the breed increased at a rapid rate throughout the British Isles. Welsh Terriers were well represented in large English shows such as Crystal Palace, Crufts and Birmingham. By 1896, Welsh Terrier breeding and show stock was being exported in increasing numbers to Germany, Belgium, South Africa, India and the US. Judges from the UK were much in demand to critique the progress of foreign breeding.

Two years after Walter Glynn purchased his first Welsh Terrier in 1887, he began judging classes at home and abroad and became a member of The Kennel Club. Dogs with his Brynhir affix became the foundation of many kennels worldwide. When Mr. Glynn died in 1933, he had owned and bred more Welsh Terrier champions than anyone else in the previous half-century.

Another breeder of note on both sides of the Atlantic was T. H. Harris of Sennybridge, whose Eng. Ch. Resiant was made up in

The Welsh Terrier as it appeared in an 1887 publication.

1895. The first champion he actually owned and made up was Nell Gwynne in 1897. His Senny affix became synonymous with top-quality Welsh Terriers.

The first woman to award Challenge Certificates to Welsh Terriers was Mrs. H. L. Aylmer in 1907 at the Bristol show. It is historically significant that she was chosen for this honor since her affix, Glansevin, came from her family ties with the Glansevin Welsh Hound Pack, noted for the Welsh Terriers that ran with it in the 1700s.

It should be noted that many Welsh Terriers in 1900 were still working terriers. By no means had they given up their day jobs for stardom! The ownership of all dogs as pets had only become acceptable and popular due to the example set by Queen Victoria. Prior to that time, royalty carried about various toy breeds, but commoners could not afford to feed a non-working animal. Dog shows took matters a step further. Those who could not afford to keep race horses, or horses and hounds for the hunt,

WELSH GRAMMAR LESSON

The Welsh alphabet does not include the letters K, J, Q, V, X or Z, but it does have six others to make up for it. It goes like this: A, B, C, CH, D, E, F, FF, G, H, I, (J only for words borrowed from English), L, LL, M, N, O, P, PH, R, RH, S, T, TH, U, W and Y.

Galen Rexus,
bred and owned
by Mr. J. S.
Gilbert, was born
in September
1930.

Kynan O' Gaint
was Mr. A. T.
Morris's dog, born
in March 1930.

could and did manage kennels of show dogs. Additionally, showing dogs held more prestige than showing livestock, although most of the early breeders had their roots in breeding sheep, rabbits or chickens to exhibit at agricultural shows. It may have been the idea that one could now take pride in selling a top show dog to a member of the aristocracy, whereas one could not hold one's head as high on the similar sale of a prize chicken!

In 1899, Princess Adolphus of Teck bought a bitch, Brynafon Nellie, and promptly became a breeder, exhibitor and ardent supporter of the Welsh Terrier Club. Then, in 1911, a group of Welsh Terrier fanciers in North Wales raised the necessary money and bought a dog for HRH The Prince of Wales. The rest of that story reads like pure fiction. The bitch was Queen Llechwedd (called Gwen), sired by Dewi Sant (St. David, patron saint of Wales). The following year (1912) His Royal Highness registered two pups whelped on March 1, St. David's Day.

Gochel Fi, owned by Mrs. O. Jones, was born in 1926. This fine Welsh Terrier beat three breed champions in the show ring.

Serendipity continued to be on the side of the Welsh, although until the 1920s the controversy continued with articles referring to the "so-called Welsh Terrier" and comparisons of the breed to the "beautiful" Fox Terrier. Not to worry. A new world of dogs was on the rise and pets were becoming better fed, better housed and better cared for both at home and through outstanding advances in veterinary medicine.

Eng. Ch. Delswood Welcome, born in September 1931, was bred and owned by Mr. A. H. Symonds.

DOGGIE HUBBARD LIVES ON

There is a room at the library of the University of Wales in Aberystwyth dedicated to Clifford ("Doggie") Hubbard's superb collection of books on dogs, said to be the finest and most extensive in the world.

Eng. Ch. Lady Gwen, born in August 1925, earned her champion title at the National Terrier and Kennel Club Championship Shows. She was exported to Germany.

THE WELSH GAINS FAME

Joe Hitchings's Aman kennels in the Rhondda Valley were a dominant force in the breed after World War I and largely contributed to the area's being called "the whelping box of the Welsh Terrier." Hitchings handled many breeds but is best remembered for putting a modern stamp on the Welsh Terrier.

Eng. Ch. Senny Rex, owned by Mr. T. H. Harris, was born in 1925.

Hitchings, along with Sam Warburton in England and George Steadman Thomas (who was in effect a trans-Atlantic commuter) were responsible for sending a steady supply of quality Welsh Terriers to American kennels. With dogs being lined up on one side of the ocean and Welsh Terrier enthusiasts eagerly awaiting their arrival on the other, the stage was set for the breed's solid future in the modern world.

There were numerous true terriermen at this time. Hitchings continued breeding Welsh Terriers for 42 years. Arthur Harris (Ronvale), T. H. Harris (Senny) and A. E. Harris (Penhill) also remained in the breed for close to half a century. Harold Snow's Felstead kennels were continued by his son Emlyn and grandson Lyn: three generations of dedication to the breed.

After World War II, the breed's popularity skyrocketed and names such as Mervin Pickering (Groveview), Dai Rees (Ebbw Swell), Cyril Williams (Caiach) and Phil Thomas (Sandstorm) came to the forefront. There were two prestigious wins in this period to boost the breed dramatically. The Crufts Best in Show winner in 1951 was Ch. Twynstar Dyma Fi; in 1959, Ch. Sandstorm Saracen repeated the feat, handled by his breeder, Mr. Thomas. It wasn't until 1994 that another Welsh Terrier was to claim the same honor, this time Ch. Purston Hit and Miss From Brocolitia, bred by Michael Collings and owned by Mrs. Anne J. Maughan. The next Crufts Best in Show achievement followed just four years later, by Ch. Saredon Forever Young, bred by Judy Averis and David Scawthorn.

Lord Atlee, former Prime Minister, chose his two Welsh Terriers as supporters for his coat of arms and the words *Labor omnia vincit* or "Work conquers all"—a fitting tribute to both the man and the dogs. The Welsh fashion designer Laura Ashley brought a touch of fame to the breed when her Welsh Terrier, Clem, became the subject of a series of popular children's books.

In the 20th century, registration numbers in the UK were somewhat static until a high in 1927 of 288. By 1951, due in part to the fame of Twynstar Dyma Fi, those numbers escalated to 359. They remained in the 200–300 range, but new heights of popularity are expected in this 21st century. In the US, the registrations average 700 annually.

There is always a threat to a breed such as the Welsh Terrier that inherited defects will become magnified in their small gene pool or that the overall quality will diminish. Fortunately for the breed, as import-export laws have been relaxed and the use of frozen semen increased, sound Welsh Terrier breeding stock is more easily obtainable worldwide.

ABOUT THE WTA

In 1923, the Welsh Terrier Association (WTA) was founded in England, becoming the second club for the breed. The year prior, an older club, the South Wales Welsh Terrier Breeders' Association, which had been the breed's second club, joined up

Eng. Ch. Hold Up, owned by A. E. Harris, was born in 1925 and won many Challenge Certificates at important shows.

A PINT FOR BEST OF BREED?
Some of the first gatherings of dog owners, the precursors of today's dog shows, took place in pubs. Everyone in the pub became judge, exhibitor and spectator, all going over the dogs and giving their opinions.

Ch. Bardwyn Bronze Bertram, bred by author Bardi McLennan. He was a top producing sire with 25 champions to his credit.

with the Welsh Terrier Club (WTC), the original club for the breed. A good portion of British breed fanciers today belong to both clubs. In 1970, the WTA began a most informative and well-organized yearbook, reflecting the Welsh Terriers in Britain and in foreign lands. On June 1, 1980, this club held its first Open Show at the home of George and Olive Jackson (Jokyl), with 39 dogs in 88 entries. Judged by Beryl Blower (Turith), Best in Show was awarded to Mr. Jenkins and Miss Nock's Ch. Bowers Princess, handled by Ray Davies.

In 1981, when the Welsh Terrier Club was granted permission to award Challenge Certifi-

MADOC AT BAY

One of perhaps the wildest of Celtic claims concerned a Prince Madoc, who was said to have crossed the Atlantic Ocean and landed in what is now Mobile Bay, Alabama in 1170. The legend was endorsed by Queen Elizabeth in 1580, no doubt due in some large part to pressure from her science advisor and magician, John Dee, who was—of course—a Welshman!

acknowledge this stalwart club's standing; perhaps they never asked. The top Welsh Terrier in Britain that year and the following was Mr. Jenkins and Miss Nock's Ch. Puzzle of Kenstaff, bred by R. Ogles. This lovely bitch won Best of Breed at Crufts and Best in Show at the National Terrier Specialty.

cates, club president Mrs. Margaret Thomas was asked to judge the premier event. It is difficult to imagine why it took 95 years for The Kennel Club to

MADE UP IN AMERICA

Not surprisingly, the largest population of Welsh Terriers today is in the United States. The Welsh's rise in popularity began

Ch. Kirkwood Brazen Overture, bred and owned by Ann Baumgardner and Judith Ford Anspach, winning Best of Breed at Westminster Kennel Club in 2004.

when a young dog named Nigwood Nailer won a 30-guinea Challenge Cup in the UK for Best Welsh, Irish or Fox Terrier in Show in 1899 and was immediately bought up by Major Carnochan and brought to America. The following year, the Welsh Terrier Club of America was formed, with Major Carnochan as treasurer. Nigwood Nailer went on to become the first Welsh Terrier to become an American Kennel Club champion, which he did in 1903.

The Misses Beatrice and Gertrude de Coppet were to be the backbone of the breed club from 1900 until 1960. The sisters' Windermere kennels were among the first to be devoted solely to the Welsh Terrier, based on dogs imported from T. H. Harris in 1890. The ladies were always attired in hats and white kennel coats while handling their own dogs, and they could be quite intimidating in the show ring. Among numerous contributions to the club, Beatrice de Coppet designed the club logo.

Over the ensuing years in the US, many people and dogs established the Welsh Terrier as a

Ch. Hapitails Hit Parade, bred by co-owner Elizabeth Leaman and Richard Powell, co-owned with Jill and Peter See, was number-one Welsh in 2003 with multiple Bests in Show.

A team from Russia's zo Strelki kennel, winning Best Breeders Group at the Novgorod, Russia show. Novgorod is home to several Welsh Terrier breeders, and interest in the breed is high in that area.

worthy challenger in the Terrier Group. From the 1940s through the 1970s, kennel affixes such as Halcyon, Strathglass, Twin Ponds, Coltan, Pool Forge, Licken Run, Penzance and Tujays became staples of the breed. In more recent years, such names as Anasazi, Sunspryte, Hapitails, Kirkwood, Cisseldale and Czar came to the forefront. That is not to say that the imported dogs are lagging behind. Imports keep arriving and doing a fair share of winning.

Of special note are three Welsh Terriers bred by Michael and Nancy O'Neal of New Mexico. Each of them has earned a place in the record books. Ch. Anasazi Annie Oakley took her place as top-winning Welsh Terrier bitch with 40 Bests in

Show and 106 Terrier Group wins. Ch. Anasazi Trail Boss topped the stud record with 60 champion get and Ch. Anasazi Billy The Kid retired in 1999 after breaking all Welsh Terrier records with 100 Bests in Show and over 150 Group Firsts. An amazing feat from a small kennel!

THE WORLD OF THE WELSH
In many countries on the Continent, dogs must still prove that they can perform the tasks for which they were originally bred. As late as 1990 at the World Dog Show in the former Czechoslovakia, Welsh Terriers were a novelty as show dogs to people from Poland, Russia, East Germany and what is now the Czech Republic and Slovakia, but the breeders were charmed by the dogs' presence in the show ring, and the breed is making great strides in these countries. In Russia, a team of seven Welsh Terriers from zo Strelki kennels won the Breeders Group at a show near Novgorod—and very

Shaireab's Honor Among Thieves, known to friends as "Stuart," is owned by Sharon Abmeyer.

BELOW: Crufts winner the successful Eng. Ch. Purston Hit and Miss from Brocolitia.

nice specimens they were. Welsh Terriers are still primarily working earthdogs in Russia, and in Poland they are actually the breed of choice for hunting.

GERMANY

The first classes for Welsh Terriers in Germany were at the Berlin show in 1896. Today the breed is in good shape with several dedicated breeders such as Mr. Axel Mohrke, who has exported his Bismarckquelle dogs worldwide. Mrs. Irmatraud Becker (v. Ganseliesel) is another breeder with top-winning dogs.

DENMARK
Both the Borchorst and the El-Fri-Ba kennels are at the top of the breed in Denmark. Their Welsh Terrier stock has traveled as far as America and Australia.

FINLAND
Registrations of the breed in Finland were on a downturn until quite recently. Due in great part to the success of Sari Mäkëla's Vicway dogs, things are looking up for the breed. Ch. Vicway Live Free Or Die, a son of Multi-Ch. Vicway Live and Let Die (a dog sired by Ch. High Flyer's Welsh Baron), was a World Winner in 1998. Participation in agility has a slight edge over participation in conformation shows.

SWEDEN
Sweden has been involved with the Welsh Terrier since dog shows began in that country. The late Per Thorsen (Snowdonia) played a leading role in establishing the popularity of the breed. Lars Adenheimer (Aden) is yet another Welsh Terrier breeder whose kennel affix is recognized everywhere.

The Swedish law against tail-docking not only has hurt the importing of dogs for the show ring but also has prevented Welsh Terriers with docked tails from competing in dog shows as well as agility, obedience or other such events. A recent World Show held in Sweden drew much criticism from owners of dogs that were disqualified for this reason, when the docking of tails is still legal (but not mandatory) in the breed's land of origin.

FRANCE
Mesdames Remy and Bernaudin of France owned the Best in Show Felstead Formulate and later purchased Ch. Solentine Sugar Ray, a dog bred by Wendy Gatto-Ronchieri that was top stud dog in Britain in 1995.

HOLLAND
Holland is fortunate to have one of the world's top breeders, Jan

A junior handler winning a high award at an International Championship Show in Holland, under an American judge.

Albers, whose High Flyer Welsh Terriers have a definite stamp, a unique look. Many High Flyer dogs are top winners and producers and have been the foundation of other kennels on the Continent and overseas.

BRITAIN

Among the kennels of note today in the UK are Felstead, Philtown, Serenfach, Alokin, Davannadot, Saredon, Glyncastle and Wigmore. The breed is in excellent form in its native land with a steady growth of new breeders and exhibitors smitten by the Welsh Terrier.

PURE-BRED PURPOSE

Given the vast range of the world's 400 or so pure breeds of dog, it's fair to say that domestic dogs are the most versatile animal in the kingdom. From the tiny 1-pound lap dog to the 200-pound guard dog, dogs have adapted to every need and whim of their human masters. Humans have selectively bred dogs to alter physical attributes like size, color, leg length, mass and skull diameter in order to suit our own needs and fancies. Dogs serve humans not only as companions and guardians but also as hunters, exterminators, shepherds, rescuers, messengers, warriors, babysitters and more!

The late Frank Kellett handled Ch. Purston Hit and Miss from Brocolitia to Best in Show at Crufts in 1994. He is shown with owner Anne Maughan.

CHARACTERISTICS OF THE
WELSH TERRIER

WHY THE WELSH TERRIER?
Sometimes one has to wonder if perchance the Welsh Terrier speaks only Welsh, for the dog has an uncanny knack of ignoring directions and commands given in the owner's native tongue. This is often mistaken for stubbornness, but that's not quite true. The Welsh Terrier is easily distracted and therefore may not be paying attention to you, or, more accurately, is paying strict attention to something else. That's the contradictory nature of the Welsh Terrier—easily distracted or intensely focused, which is, after all, how an earthdog must function. Take your eye off the target (be it rat, fox or badger) and you've lost the "game"!

A similar scenario mistaken for obstinacy occurs when the dog is asked to obey a command that he has demonstrated over and over again that he can perform perfectly. Being a sensible dog, the Welsh Terrier sees nothing to be gained by pointless repetition.

The breed is intelligent and, as everyone knows, it isn't always easy to cope with intelligence. He

is not a canine robot, but instead will show you (without having been asked) just how many different ways he can execute your request. It may be amusing to watch his mental wheels go round, and no harm is done so long as you remain amiably in control. The Welsh Terrier may have coined the phrase "equal opportunity employer," for he will seize every opportunity to become your equal, or better. If you drop your role as leader, rest assured that your Welsh friend will retrieve it instantly. The Welsh Terrier is an intelligent, alert dog and great fun to teach basic obedience and home rules, even if a bit of a challenge.

TRAINABILITY
Begin as you mean to continue. Training begins from the moment the puppy (or adult) steps across the threshold of your household. Undeniably the best training method is bribery and coercion. Well, at least bribery! Later in this book, it is more politely referred to as "positive reinforcement," which means whenever the dog

All terriers are curious, active and easily distracted—are your family and home ready for a Welsh?

does as he's told, you hand out tiny food rewards. When he does not, you accept the fact that you did not properly explain what you wanted him to do, and you begin again. An occasional "No!" is permissible, with an exaggerated frown to signify your total displeasure. Physical punishment is definitely not acceptable and might even encourage reciproca-tion in kind. Welsh Terriers do not have strong jaws and large teeth for naught! It is wise not to become involved in trading smacks for bites.

House-training a Welsh Terrier is seldom a problem when a consistent schedule is followed, ample praise is given for relieving himself where he should and the dog is confined when no one is free to keep an eye on him.

WITH YOUNGSTERS

A question often asked is how the breed gets along with children.

There are two answers. The Welsh Terrier is very good with slightly older children; he is ready to obey them and ready for almost any game they want to play, even agreeing to be dressed up! However, a Welsh puppy is not a suitable new pet to consider for families with babies or children under the age of five years. The puppy will treat these little ones as littermates, and if you've ever watched a litter of pups in action, you know that needle-sharp puppy teeth are invariably involved in play. Small children who have never had a puppy can't be expected to understand.

Speaking of babies, it should be pointed out that the Welsh Terrier, regardless of age, is not a baby and should never be treated like one. He is a dog, knows he's a dog and, what's more, is proud to be one. He's also a terrier, which makes him a bit more of a dog if that's possible!

THE BEST HOME

Given a choice, Welsh Terriers would no doubt prefer to live in the country, but will settle down contentedly if an apartment in the city is where his family will be. In any home with any type of yard or outdoor area, a fence is essen-tial for the dog's safety in today's world of busy streets and traffic, even in residential areas. The breed is not given to excessive or senseless barking, which is a

A well-behaved child and an equally well-behaved Welsh Terrier make a wonderful pair.

blessing to both owners and neighbors, no matter where you live.

The hunting instincts of the breed make walks more than a mere stroll down the lane. A brisk 30-minute walk with frequent stops for sniffing, exploring, tracking and greeting passers-by (human and canine) is ideal. Twice a day would be lovely. Once will suffice if augmented by periods of vigorous play, such as games of fetch.

The Welsh Terrier is a calm housedog, not given to boisterous behavior when adequately exercised. Most will alert you to a car or pedestrian coming up the path, but, to be honest, they are more likely to sound the alarm at an invasion by the neighbor's cat. Welsh Terriers raised with cats are generally tolerant of them, although one cannot always say the same for the cats! Introducing a cat into the home of an older Welsh who is unfamiliar with felines is another matter entirely. Proceed with utmost caution.

NOT QUITE PERFECT

As a Welsh Terrier owner, you may run into a behavioral problem based on something no one warned you about. It is called the Welsh Terrier Code of Ownership: "What's mine is mine and if I have any part of it (or anything else) in my mouth, that's mine, too!" It's rather like

dealing with a child in the "terrible twos" stage! I don't mean to make light of it, however, for it can develop into aggressive behavior in an otherwise very compliant dog. It is not a game; you are dealing with a true terrier.

Never try to snatch anything away from the Welsh. You could be bitten in his attempt merely to hang onto his prize. Nor should you ever attempt to crawl under a bed or table to pull him out in order to retrieve your socks. Not only will you meet those jaws again, but you are confronting an earthdog. When he retreats into a small dark place with something he caught (well, "stole" is more accurate), he is in his totally natural element and will breach no mortal meddling in his domain.

The most you might achieve is a terrier battle of wits with the unpleasant sound of growling and the unacceptable appearance of curled lips and menacing teeth. The dog's owner needs to realize that he is actually causing the dog to react in this way. Let's say it's unacceptable behavior on the part of the human.

How to avoid such confrontation? Easily, by the simple means of prevention. The day your Welsh Terrier enters your home, begin to teach "drop it" or "give it" by offering a tiny treat in your left hand while holding out your right hand to accept the surrendered toy. Food is always more desirable than a mere toy or even a stolen object. As with all training, gradually diminish the use of treats, but do keep up a verbal "Good dog." This clever trick could save the dog's life when he picks up a poisonous object (or makes off with your leather purse). Lure him out of hiding with a treat worth his while—a bit of cheese or sausage, for example.

Aggressive behavior in any dog is dangerous. In the Welsh Terrier, as in any other terrier, it is compounded by the dog's natural speed and the strength of his jaws. Luckily for us (and for the dogs), this turn of events is easily preventable in the normally good-natured Welsh Terrier.

Remember that Welsh Terriers are, above all, intelligent. They study and understand our body language more clearly than our words. Therefore the exaggerated frown is a big help in relaying your message of disapproval. Welsh Terriers are also gluttons for treats and can be persuaded by food to do almost anything. If you ever hear a growl or a snarl, say "No" with a big frown. Then quickly give the dog a familiar command like "Sit," to which you can say "Good dog" and give a reward. Gradually the food can be eliminated and verbal praise alone will be effective.

THE LASTING LOVE OF A WELSH

The Welsh Terrier is eager and able to take on whatever lifestyle is asked of him. He will be equally adept as a lap dog, foot warmer or

HEART-HEALTHY

In this modern age of ever-improving cardio-care, no doctor or scientist can dispute the advantages of owning a dog to lower a person's risk of heart disease. Studies have proven that petting a dog, walking a dog and grooming a dog all show positive results toward lowering your blood pressure. The simple routine of exercising your dog—going outside with the dog and walking, jogging or playing catch—is heart-healthy in and of itself. If you are normally less active than your physician thinks you should be, adopting a dog may be a smart option to improve your own quality of life as well as that of another creature.

companion to an elderly person, or, for the more active, as a hiking, hunting, swimming or boating partner. An interesting phenomenon about the Welsh Terrier is how faithful people are to the breed. Adults who grew up with Welsh Terriers invariably want the same breed for their children, and another when those children leave home and still another for their retirement years.

These small black and tan terriers have a unique way of fitting into each phase of our lives with charm, personality and sensible companionship that elicit an extreme loyalty in their owners. Airedale owners who, in their later years, can no longer cope with the size and strength of that breed, switch in great numbers to the Welsh. Then they often have to respond to that persistently annoying query, "Is that a miniature Airedale?" with a somewhat defiant, "No, sir (or ma'am). It is a Welsh Terrier!"

GOOD HEALTH

A genetically sound Welsh Terrier fed a good canine diet and given sufficient exercise and routine visits to the vet will live 12 to 15 years in good health. There are no health problems that are breed-specific, but certain problems that can be seen in all dogs, pure-bred and mixed, do occur now and then in the Welsh. Buying from a breeder with a good reputation for sound stock is the best way to avoid such genetic disorders as glaucoma, lens luxation, epilepsy, hypothyroidism and skin allergies, which can affect the Welsh.

There is no way to guarantee a lifetime free of all illness for any individual dog, but usually Welsh Terriers are a healthy, hardy lot. The explanation for this good fortune may lie in the fact that the breed has never become overly popular. Working with small numbers, dedicated breeders are quickly aware of any genetically transmitted disease and thus are able to remove affected animals from their breeding programs.

ADDITIONAL ACCOMPLISHMENTS

While the reader has been taken through many of the charming ways in which a Welsh Terrier can usurp authority, it is not always a battle of wits. Here's a look at other uses for both his terrier tenacity and common sense.

THERAPY DOGS

As therapy dogs, Welsh Terriers are quite astonishing to behold. They quickly sense what is expected of them and become calm, almost serene, moving slowly and confidently among the ill and aged. They are unafraid of wheelchairs or walkers, and are willing to be petted by unsteady hands.

AGILITY TRIALS

Agility must have been made for terriers! All those obstacles, jumps and tunnels are second nature to the Welsh Terrier's physical stamina, sense of adventure and natural terrier instincts. To be realistic, however, getting him to cover the course in the required order is another matter entirely. Halfway through the tunnel, he may decide to wait for a fox to appear! However, do not despair. Keep your sense of humor and enjoy his amusing behavior.

THE EARTHDOG

The reason these dogs were put on earth is—the *earth*! That is, to go to ground, and how they know it! Nothing can compare with the total body expression of a Welsh Terrier—eyes, ears, neck, tail—fired up by the smells of the earth, the natural hunting instinct put to the test. It makes little difference if the hunt is a natural one in the fields or along riverbanks, or in one of the artificial earths used in many earthdog tests with protected vermin (usually rats) to assess and maintain the working capabilities of the terriers. The Welsh Terrier is in his element and relishes the activity. Yet, on returning home, your friend will curl up near you by the fire, completely content.

Terrier means "earth dog"...and any Welsh welcomes the opportunity to put his paws to work!

THE DELIGHTFUL DOG OF WALES

It's difficult to sum up these delightful Welsh dogs, because they can be so diverse in personality and in the roles they play in our individual lives. I've tried to give you the bad along with the good, lest you think these black and tans belong on a pedestal. Indeed, they have their feet firmly on the ground with a heavenly, very high opinion of themselves.

It is useful to keep in mind that these dogs come from Wales, a country known for a folk tradition of argument or debate; perhaps the Welsh Terrier is carrying on that tradition. The dog is strong willed (anything weaker would be no match for his natural prey), but with enough common sense to know when it is wiser to follow the rules. For that reason alone, the owner of a Welsh Terrier must be something of a Welsh Terrier himself, able to understand the debate but also able always to remain in charge.

BREED STANDARD FOR THE

WELSH TERRIER

One initial obstacle for dog historians was the breeders' reluctance to use originality in naming their dogs. Literally hundreds of Welsh Terrier bitches named either Fan or Nell were further identified only occasionally by the owner's name. And how many Joneses would you guess there are in Wales? Since dogs changed owners from one show to the next, it was almost impossible to keep track of all the Fans and Nells. Major P. F. Brine took on the task of putting together a stud book for Britain's Welsh Terrier Club with records going back to 1854. He completed this herculean work in 1903.

Once founded, the Welsh Terrier Club (WTC) immediately set about drawing up a breed standard, which it completed in 1895. The first dog-show breeders and judges were stockmen and horsemen whose great knowledge was based on the working aspects of their animals. "Form follows function" was the rule and the reason why the original standard did not include the obvious. It remained unchanged until 1948, when the

breed height was raised from 15 to 15.5 inches, a decision arrived at jointly by the WTC and the Welsh Terrier Association (WTA). The format in which the English standard appears today was approved by The Kennel Club in 1994.

The Kennel Club standard was used in the US until 1984, when parts of it were rewritten in an effort to translate it into "American English." To assist new breeders unfamiliar with breed vernacular, the Welsh Terrier Club of America publishes an annotated standard, "The Welsh Terrier in Profile," which explains the standard in detail and with sketches of each portion of the standard.

The standard is the blueprint or written description of the perfect dog of that breed, and thus serves to train the breeder's eye. It serves as a quick reference sheet for the show judge. Although one cannot quarrel with obvious deviations from it, nevertheless every breed standard is open to subjective interpretation. One person may wish to forgive a slightly gay tail and focus instead on the lovely head, while another observer sees that gay tail as a major defect, taking precedence over the nice head.

In judging the Welsh Terrier, whether by qualified conformation judges, breeders or ringside spectators, the emphasis must be on the working aspect of the dog and thus on soundness, not mere beauty. A dog with a weak front or hindquarters, or one with too short a back, or with a quarrelsome temperament, could not perform a productive day's work.

The lovely alert eye and ear expression of a Welsh Terrier, combined with good ears and set-on of tail, are the beauty aspects of the dog, referred to as "type." Soundness and type must be considered jointly to be judged against that unattainable perfect specimen as described in the standard.

Mr. Walter Glynn's description is as valid today as when he wrote it 100 years ago: "The Welsh Terrier is built on the lines of a powerful, short-legged, short-backed hunter. He is best with a jet black back and neck, and deep tan head, ears, legs and tail; ears a shade deeper than elsewhere." You will note that soundness is foremost.

The most notable change in the Welsh Terrier seen from pictures of the early show dogs to those of the present is the acquisition of face and leg furnishings (the profusion of fuzzy hair on those parts). Since no farmer or miner of the day would have bothered to pluck out the hair in these areas, it is apparent that the breed originally had little or no excess hair on the legs or muzzle. The furnishings came about with the beauty aspect of the dog shows. It wasn't until the late 1920s and '30s that these were considered essential parts of the Welsh Terrier's show coat. Welsh Terriers in the US have their facial furnishings trimmed and shaped for the show ring. In Britain and on the Continent, the Welsh Terrier is shown in a somewhat more natural, or workmanlike, state.

THE AMERICAN KENNEL CLUB BREED STANDARD FOR THE WELSH TERRIER

General Appearance: The Welsh Terrier is a sturdy, compact, rugged dog of medium size with a coarse wire-textured coat. The legs, underbody and head are tan;

A head study illustrating correct type.

A male Welsh Terrier of correct type and balance.

the jacket black (or occasionally grizzle). The tail is docked to length meant to complete the image of a "square dog" approximately as high as he is long. The movement is a terrier trot typical of the long-legged terrier. It is effortless, with good reach and drive. The Welsh Terrier is friendly, outgoing to people and other dogs, showing spirit and courage. The "Welsh Terrier expression" comes from the set, color and position of the eyes combined with the use of the ears.

Size, Proportion, Substance: Males are about 15 inches at the withers, with an acceptable range between 15 and 15.5. Bitches may be proportionally smaller. Twenty pounds is considered an average weight, varying a few pounds depending on the height of the dog and the density of bone. Both dog and bitch appear solid and of good substance.

Head: The entire head is rectangular. The *eyes* are small, dark brown and almond-shaped, well set in the skull. They are placed fairly far apart. The size, shape, color and position of the eyes give the steady, confident but alert expression that is typical of the Welsh Terrier. The *ears* are V-shaped, small, but not too thin.

The fold is just above the topline of the skull. The ears are carried forward close to the cheek with the tips falling to, or toward, the outside corners of the eyes when the dog is at rest. The ears move slightly up and forward when at attention. *Skull*—The foreface is strong with powerful, punishing jaws. It is only slightly narrower than the backskull. There is a slight stop. The backskull is of equal length to the foreface. They are on parallel planes in profile.

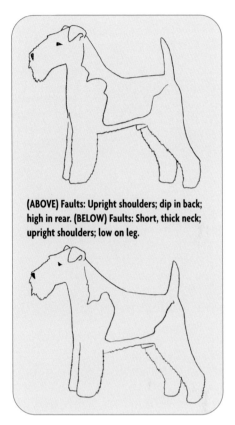

(ABOVE) Faults: Upright shoulders; dip in back; high in rear. (BELOW) Faults: Short, thick neck; upright shoulders; low on leg.

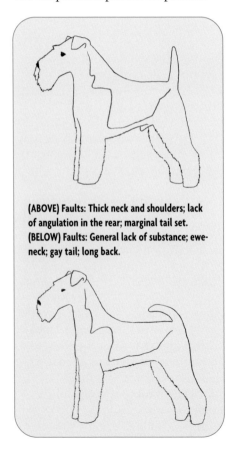

(ABOVE) Faults: Thick neck and shoulders; lack of angulation in the rear; marginal tail set. (BELOW) Faults: General lack of substance; ewe-neck; gay tail; long back.

The backskull is smooth and flat (not domed) between the ears. There are no wrinkles between the ears. The cheeks are flat and clean (not bulging). The *muzzle* is one-half the length of the entire head from tip of nose to occiput. The foreface in front of the eyes is well made up. The furnishings on the foreface are trimmed to complete without exaggeration the total rectangular outline. The muzzle is strong and squared off, never snipy. The nose is black and

Comparing type in the Welsh (LEFT) and Wire-haired Fox Terrier (RIGHT). The Welsh is stockier, with more substance. The Fox Terrier has a longer, narrower head, with smaller, high-set ears.

squared off. The lips are black and tight. A scissors bite is preferred, but a level bite is acceptable. Either one has complete dentition. The teeth are large and strong, set in powerful, vise-like jaws.

Neck, Topline, Body: The neck is of moderate length and thickness, slightly arched and sloping gracefully into the shoulders. The throat is clean with no excess of skin. The topline is level. The body shows good substance and is well ribbed up. There is good depth of brisket and moderate width of chest. The loin is strong and moderately short. The tail is docked to a length approximately level (on an imaginary line) with the occiput, to complete the square image of the whole dog. The root of the tail is set well up on the back. It is carried upright.

Forequarters: The front is straight. The shoulders are long, sloping and well laid back. The legs are straight and muscular with upright and powerful

pasterns. The feet are small, round, and catlike. The pads are thick and black. The nails are strong and black; any dewclaws are removed.

Hindquarters: The hindquarters are strong and muscular with well-developed second thighs and the stifles well bent. The hocks are moderately straight, parallel and short from joint to ground. The feet should be the same as in the forequarters.

Coat: The coat is hard, wiry, and dense with a close-fitting thick jacket. There is a short, soft undercoat. Furnishings on muzzle, legs, and quarters are dense and wiry.

Color: The jacket is black, spreading up onto the neck, down onto the tail and into the upper thighs. The legs, quarters, and head are clear tan. The tan is a deep reddish color, with slightly lighter shades acceptable. A grizzle jacket is also acceptable.

Ch. Shaireab's Sam I Am, owned by Sharon Abmeyer, finished his championship from the puppy classes. Sam is producing good bone, excellent movement and lovely headpieces.

Gait: The movement is straight, free and effortless, with good reach in front, strong drive behind, with feet naturally tending to converge toward a median line of travel as speed increases.

Temperament: The Welsh Terrier is a game dog—alert, aware, spirited, but at the same time, is friendly and shows self control. Intelligence and desire to please are evident in his attitude. A specimen exhibiting an overly aggressive attitude, or shyness, should be penalized.

Faults: Any deviation from the foregoing should be considered a fault; the seriousness of the fault depending upon the extent of the deviation.

Approved August 10, 1993
Effective September 29, 1993

Am-Int. Ch. Kirkwood Top Brass, owned by Frank Stevens, was a Montgomery County and Westminster Best of Breed winner. He is the sire of Group and specialty winners.

WELSH TERRIER

SIGNS OF A HEALTHY PUPPY

Healthy puppies are robust little fellows who are alert and active, sporting shiny coats and supple skin. They should not appear lethargic, bloated or pot-bellied, nor should they have flaky skin or runny or crusted eyes or noses. Their stools should be firm and well formed, with no evidence of blood or mucus.

SELECTING A PUPPY

You'll notice a few things when taking your first look at a Welsh litter. If you see the Welsh pups at three or four weeks of age, they are likely to be almost entirely black. However, the tan increases in all the right places as the pups mature. Also, don't worry if the dam is a bit protective of her brood; that's normal.

Nine to ten weeks is the ideal age to bring a Welsh puppy into your life. Each puppy needs that much time to learn that he is a dog, how to behave as a dog and—so very importantly—how to read the body language of other dogs. A misunderstanding in the latter is usually the spark that sets off a fight. The Welsh can best learn all of this from his dam and littermates. The physical, and sometimes vocal, activity among littermates is part of the essential learning experience.

Unless you have previously owned a Welsh Terrier, know something about the breed and consider yourself to be a "terrier person," I would not advise you to select the most active pup in

FINDING A QUALIFIED BREEDER

Before you begin your puppy search, ask for references from the breed club, your veterinarian and other breeders to refer you to someone they believe is reputable. Responsible breeders usually raise only one or two breeds of dog. Avoid any breeder who has several different breeds or has several litters at the same time. Dedicated breeders are usually involved with a breed or other dog club. Many participate in some sport or activity related to their breed. Just as you want to be assured of the breeder's qualifications, the breeder wants to be assured that you will make a worthy owner. Expect the breeder to interview you, asking questions about your goals for the pup, your experience with dogs and what kind of home you will provide.

a look that says, "See me? I'm the best!" That one may be destined for the show ring, or could be a nice pet with a good attitude. A calm, somewhat quiet puppy may be sizing you up as a potential partner. At the other end of the temperament scale is the shy

Bring the family along when visiting the litter. Everyone should take part in selecting the new puppy.

the litter. In some breeds, that would be exactly the pup to choose, but not in the Welsh Terrier. The one that wants to continue to play energetically when the others stop is not going to be an easy pup to convince that he must take his orders from you! He will need a pleasant but very firm, very consistent hand to tone down his natural exuberance, which otherwise will turn into dominance.

There is also the pup that looks you straight in the eye with

pup. True shyness is almost unheard of in Welsh Terriers, so beware the pup that shuns your hand or creeps away to sit by himself. That one may require the help of a professional behaviorist before too long.

CREATE A SCHEDULE
Puppies thrive on sameness and routine. Offer meals at the same time each day, take him out at regular times for potty trips and do the same for play periods and outdoor activity. Make note of when your puppy naps and when he is most lively and energetic, and try to plan his day around those times. Once he is house-trained and more predictable in his habits, he will be better able to tolerate changes in his schedule.

Choose any one of the happy, friendly, normal Welsh pups wanting to kiss your hands, nibble your fingers or just have your attention. The chances are good that you won't even be confronted with either of the two extremes.

PUPPY NEEDS AND DEVELOPMENT
Your Welsh Terrier puppy will need all-day everyday attention for about six weeks. The routine of feeding, house-training and exercise is broken only by frequent naps (yours coinciding with the pup's). If you are not there to teach the puppy what he can do (as well as where and when) and what he cannot ever do, he will instantly teach himself. If he gets away with something naughty because nobody was there to tell him otherwise, the puppy will have taught himself that it was the right thing to do. And he'll do it again. The owner is the teacher, guidance counselor and corrections officer!

At any time between five and seven months, a Welsh Terrier may go through what is commonly called a fear phase, when the normally outgoing, happy pup may suddenly seem shy or fearful. The phase can last a day or a few weeks and the best way to live through it is not to give in to it. Keep the pup with you (on lead, if necessary) and go about your business, using a normal tone of voice and lots of

PEDIGREE VS. REGISTRATION CERTIFICATE

Too often new owners are confused between these two important documents. Your puppy's pedigree, essentially a family tree, is a written record of a dog's genealogy of three generations or more. The pedigree will show you the names as well as performance titles of all dogs in your pup's background. Your breeder must provide you with a registration application, with his part properly filled out. You must complete the application and send it to the AKC with the proper fee. Every puppy must come from a litter that has been AKC-registered by the breeder, born in the US and from a sire and dam that are also registered with the AKC.

The seller must provide you with complete records to identify the puppy. The AKC requires that the seller provide the buyer with the following: breed; sex, color and markings; date of birth; litter number (when available); names and registration numbers of the parents; breeder's name; and date sold or delivered.

cuddling your puppy and saying "It's all okay" because it most decidedly is not so in the pup's mind. Use the cheerful chat distraction routine, add some toys and turn up the TV.

After giving you all of this advice, however, the vast majority of Welsh Terriers do not go through this phase for more than five minutes. It may be due to their conviction that they will all grow up to be Airedales! Although the Welsh reaches full height by ten months of age, he is not fully mature and in fact will probably begin a period of teenage nonsense. By the age of two years, he will be a self-confident adult.

INDOOR/OUTDOOR

A Welsh Terrier is not a dog to be left outdoors despite his harsh coat and hardy physique. He

Outdoors on a rainy day is no place for the family dog. Your Welsh is a rugged outdoorsman, but he thrives on the companionship of his family and the comforts of home.

cheerful chat. Ask your guests to pay no attention until the pup makes the first overture. All of this is nature's way of cautioning the rapidly maturing puppy to slow down. Fear of thunderstorms is quite different. That is nature's way of telling all animals to seek shelter. Don't fall into the trap of

thrives on social interaction with his family and craves the creature comforts of his home. If you don't want a dog to "help" make the beds, rearrange the flowers or read a book tucked up close to you, forget the Welsh. He won't be underfoot, just close by because he is certain that you'll need his assistance at any minute.

IF YOU'D PREFER AN ADULT

If you do not have the time needed to teach a puppy all he must learn, there are several ways to obtain an adult Welsh Terrier. Breeders often have dogs or bitches that have finished their show or breeding careers—or perhaps never lived up to their potential. There are also dogs in need of adoption for any number of reasons, such as the death of a previous owner or an irresponsible, impulsive owner's abandonment. Contact the Welsh Terrier club nearest you and follow their advice. Welsh Terrier rescuers also take in abandoned dogs and dogs who end up in shelters and work hard to find loving homes for them.

The only caveat is that the adult was trained, rightly or wrongly, by someone else. The adult Welsh coming into a new home will have all the basic things to learn, such as your house rules, the family members, your home routine, the words you use, the sounds, smells and sights. He will also have an equal

NEW RELEASES

Most Welsh Terrier breeders release their puppies between nine and ten weeks of age. A breeder who allows puppies to leave the litter at five or six weeks of age may be more concerned with profit than with the puppies' welfare. However, some breeders of show or working breeds may hold one or more top-quality puppies longer, occasionally until three or four months of age, in order to evaluate the puppies' career or show potential and decide which one(s) they will keep for themselves.

amount to unlearn, including habits that you may not permit in your home. Welsh Terriers are not one-man dogs, although they are skilled at making each of their owners think otherwise. There will be an adjustment period and at some point the dog may indicate that it has been pleasant visiting with you, but now he'd like to go home. On the other hand, he may think he's landed in Heaven and never look back. Either way, as soon as he settles in, the new owner will become his best friend. As I've said, the Welsh Terrier is a very sensible dog.

DOG OR BITCH?

The prevalent view is that all males are aggressive watchdogs and all bitches will be sweet and stay close to home. This is pure fabrication! The differences in Welsh Terrier temperament and character are almost non-existent. Males are slightly larger and, properly raised, are complete gentlemen. Bitches can be very sweet and feminine—or not. Go with the individual pup that attracts you and, in either case, have your pet neutered or spayed by six months of age. It is a fallacy that such surgery will keep either sex closer to home or make your pet fat and lazy. It will restrain the hormones, however, and offers important health benefits. Only future show or breeding dogs should be kept sexually intact.

A CONFIDENT NEW OWNER

Like most of the other terriers, Welsh Terriers do best with terrier-like people. These are people who are themselves alert, ready to go and inquisitive, but calm, self-assured and sensible. This is not the breed for the meek and mild or indecisive.

By now you should understand what makes the Welsh Terrier a most unique and special dog, one that may fit nicely into your family and lifestyle. If you have contacted the Welsh Terrier Club of America, asked for breeder referrals and researched breeders, you should be able to recognize a knowledgeable and responsible Welsh Terrier breeder who cares not only about his pups but also about what kind of owner you will be. The Welsh Terrier Club of America's website

WTCA RESCUE

WTCARES, a branch of the parent club, rescues and re-homes Welsh Terriers throughout the United States. On average, 55 to 60 dogs go through the system annually. About 25 WTCA members serve as rescue volunteers. They locate and collect the dogs, groom them, take them to a veterinarian and evaluate temperament and training, in order to place each dog with a suitable new owner. The breed adjusts easily, and WTCARES usually has a waiting list of potential owners, carefully screened by the chairperson.

(http://clubs.akc.org/wtca) holds a wealth of information on the breed, including breeder information, health, living with a Welsh, etc. WTCA member breeders are obliged to follow a strict code of ethics in their breeding programs.

If you have completed the final step in your journey, you have found a litter, or possibly two, of quality Welsh Terrier pups. A visit with the puppies and their breeder should be an education in itself. Breed research, breeder selection and puppy visitation are very important aspects of finding the puppy of your dreams. Beyond that, these things also lay the foundation for a successful future with your pup. Puppy personalities

Visiting the breeder's facilities says a lot about the breeder and how he cares for his dogs. View the litter, meet the other dogs on the premises, see where the dogs are kept and exercised, etc.

GETTING ACQUAINTED

When visiting a litter, ask the breeder for suggestions on how best to interact with the puppies. If possible, get right into the middle of the pack and sit down with them. Observe which pups climb into your lap and which ones shy away. Toss a toy for them to chase and bring back to you. It's easy to fall in love with the puppy who picks you, but keep your future objectives in mind before you make your final decision.

within each litter vary, from the shy and easygoing puppy to the one who is dominant and assertive, with most pups falling somewhere in between. By spending time with the puppies, you will be able to recognize certain behaviors and what these behaviors indicate about each pup's temperament. Which type of pup will complement your family dynamics is best determined by observing the puppies in action within their "pack." Your breeder's expertise and recommendations are also valuable. Although you may fall in love with a bold and brassy male, the breeder may suggest that another pup would be best for you. The breeder's experience in rearing Welsh Terrier pups and matching their temperaments with appropriate humans offers the best assurance that your pup will meet your needs and expectations.

The type of puppy that you select is just as important as your decision that the Welsh Terrier is the breed for you.

The decision to live with a Welsh Terrier is a serious commitment and not one to be taken lightly. This puppy is a living sentient being that will be dependent on you for basic survival for his entire life. Beyond the basics of survival—food, water, shelter and protection—he needs much, much more. The new pup needs love, nurturing and a proper canine education to mold him into a responsible, well-behaved canine citizen. Your Welsh Terrier's health and good manners will need consistent monitoring and regular "tune-

Chow time! Sturdy bowls and good-quality food are among the items you will need for your Welsh Terrier.

ups," so your job as a responsible dog owner will be ongoing throughout every stage of his life. If you are not prepared to accept these responsibilities and commit to them for the next 12 or more years, then you are not prepared to own a dog of any breed.

Although the responsibilities of owning a dog may at times tax your patience, the joy of living with your Welsh Terrier far outweighs the workload, and a well-mannered adult dog is worth your time and effort. Before your very eyes, your new charge will grow up to be your most loyal friend, devoted to you unconditionally.

YOUR WELSH TERRIER SHOPPING LIST

Just as expectant parents prepare a nursery for their baby, so should you ready your home for the arrival of your Welsh Terrier pup.

SELECTING FROM THE LITTER

Before you visit a litter of puppies, promise yourself that you won't fall for the first pretty face you see! Decide on your goals for your puppy—show prospect, hunting dog, obedience competitor, family companion—and then look for a puppy who displays the appropriate qualities. In most litters, there is an Alpha pup (the bossy puppy), and occasionally a shy fellow who is less confident, with the rest of the litter falling somewhere in the middle. "Middle-of-the-roaders" are safe bets for most families and novice competitors.

Durable stainless steel bowls are recommended as they will withstand the wear-and-tear of terrier teeth.

If you have the necessary puppy supplies purchased and in place before he comes home, it will ease the puppy's transition from the warmth and familiarity of his mom and littermates to the brand-new environment of his new home and human family. You will be too busy to stock up and prepare your house after your pup comes home, that's for sure! Imagine how a pup must feel upon being transported to a strange new place. It's up to you to comfort him and to let your little pup know that he is going to be happy with you.

FOOD AND WATER BOWLS
Your puppy will need separate bowls for his food and water. Stainless steel pans are generally preferred over plastic bowls since they sterilize better and pups are less inclined to chew on the metal. Heavy-duty ceramic bowls are popular, but consider how often you will have to pick up those heavy bowls. Buy adult-sized pans, as your puppy will grow into them quickly.

THE DOG CRATE
If you think that crates are tools of punishment and confinement for when a dog has misbehaved, think again. Most breeders and almost all trainers recommend a crate as the preferred house-training aid as well as for all-around puppy training and safety. Because dogs are natural den creatures that prefer cave-like environments, the benefits of crate use are many. The crate provides the puppy with his very own "safe house," a cozy place to sleep, take a break or seek comfort with a favorite toy; a travel aid to house

COST OF OWNERSHIP
The purchase price of your puppy is merely the first expense in the typical dog budget. Quality dog food, veterinary care (sickness and health maintenance), dog supplies and grooming costs will add up to big bucks every year. Can you adequately afford to support a canine addition to the family?

your dog when on the road, at motels or at the vet's office; a training aid to help teach your puppy proper toileting habits; a place of solitude when non-dog people happen to drop by and don't want a lively puppy—or even a well-behaved adult dog—saying hello or begging for their attention.

Crates come in several types, although the wire crate and the fiberglass airline-type crate are the most popular. Both are safe and your puppy will adjust to either one, so the choice is up to you. The wire crates offer better visibility for the pup as well as better ventilation. Many of the wire crates collapse for easy transport. The fiberglass crates, similar to those used by the airlines for animal transport, are sturdier and more den-like. However, the fiberglass crates do not collapse and are less ventilated than a wire crate, which can be problematic in hot weather. Some of the newer crates are made of heavy plastic mesh; they are very lightweight and fold up into slim-line suitcases. However, a mesh crate might not be suitable for a pup with manic chewing habits.

The size of the crate is another thing to consider, but for the Welsh Terrier you will only need to do so once. Buy an adult-sized crate from the outset, as the pup will soon grow into it. A crate approximately 24 inches

long by 20 inches wide by 21 inches high will last the Welsh's lifetime.

The crate begins as his special puppy place to be, and as his bed overnight with the door closed. With the door left open during the day, the crate is his den where he can put his toys and be by himself for a nap. A special feature of the crate is the travel aspect, not just for safety in the car, but when you go off visiting friends and relatives, the crate is the dog's home away from home, making him feel "at home" even when he's not. The crate is the "den" of the earthdog.

BEDDING AND CRATE PADS
Your puppy will enjoy some type of soft bedding in his "room" (the crate), something he can snuggle

The most common crate types: mesh on the left, wire on the right and fiberglass on top.

into to feel cozy and secure. Old towels or blankets are good choices for a young pup, since he may (and probably will) have a toileting accident or two in the crate or decide to chew on the bedding material. Once he is fully trained and out of the early chewing stage, you can replace the puppy bedding with a permanent crate pad if you prefer. Crate pads and other dog beds run the gamut from inexpensive to high-end doggie-designer styles, but don't splurge on the good stuff until you are sure that your puppy is reliable and won't tear it up or make a mess on it.

CRATE EXPECTATIONS

To make the crate more inviting to your puppy, you can offer him a cookie inside the crate, always keeping the crate door open so that he does not feel confined. Keep a favorite toy or two in the crate for him to play with while inside. You can also cover the crate at night with a lightweight sheet to make it more den-like and remove the stimuli of household activity. Never put him into his crate as punishment or as you are scolding him, since he will then associate his crate with negative situations and avoid going there.

In addition to a crate, your Welsh will appreciate a cozy dog bed. Be aware, though, that a wicker bed can be destroyed in short order by a chewing pup and the pieces he chews off could be harmful.

PUPPY TOYS

Just as infants and older children require objects to stimulate their minds and bodies, puppies need toys to entertain their curious brains, wiggly paws and achy teeth. A fun array of safe doggie toys will help satisfy your puppy's chewing instincts and distract him from gnawing on the leg of your antique chair or your new leather sofa. Most puppy toys are cute and look as if they would be a lot of fun, but not all are necessarily safe or good for your puppy, so use caution when you go puppy-toy shopping.

Plush squeaky toys are the earthdogs' favorites! What else is there that is soft and squashy and squeals like a cornered rat? All Welsh puppies enjoy them. Indulge your pup, but monitor all toys and get rid of any that have been chewed to divulge the stuffing or squeaker or have any small parts (eyes, etc.) in danger of becoming detached and swallowed. Some Welsh Terriers will play with a squeaky toy for years, even after it no longer squeaks.

Admittedly, others will destroy the entire toy in half an hour. If your dog is one of the latter, you'll have to forgo the squeaky variety and stick with heavy-duty rubber toys or knotted rope toys and large knucklebones.

You can make an excellent puppy teething toy out of a knotted piece of towel, dampened and put in the fridge for an hour or so. Chewing into the cold toweling relieves itchy gums caused by the new teeth's erupting and provides good exercise for the jaws. An inexpensive, beneficial toy!

The best "chewcifiers" are sturdy nylon and hard rubber bones, which are safe to gnaw on and come in sizes appropriate for all age groups and breeds. Be especially careful of natural bones, which can splinter or develop dangerous sharp edges; pups can easily swallow or choke on those bone splinters. Veterinarians often tell of surgical nightmares involving bits of splintered bone, because in addition to the danger of choking, the sharp pieces can damage the intestinal tract.

Similarly, rawhide chews, while a favorite of most dogs and puppies, can be equally dangerous. Pieces of rawhide are easily swallowed after they get soft and gummy from chewing, and dogs have been known to choke on large pieces of ingested rawhide. Rawhide chews should be offered

TEETHING TIME

All puppies chew. It's normal canine behavior. Chewing just plain feels good to a puppy, especially during the three- to five-month teething period when the adult teeth are breaking through the gums. Rather than attempting to eliminate such a strong natural chewing instinct, you will be more successful if you redirect it and teach your puppy what he may or may not chew. Correct inappropriate chewing with a sharp "No!" and offer him a chew toy, praising him when he takes it. Don't become discouraged. Chewing usually decreases after the adult teeth have come in.

only when you can supervise the puppy.

If you believe that your pup has ingested a piece of one of his toys, check his stools for the next couple of days to see if he passes the item when he defecates. At

TOYS 'R SAFE

The vast array of tantalizing puppy toys is staggering. Stroll through any pet shop or pet-supply outlet and you will see that the choices can be overwhelming. However, not all dog toys are safe or sensible. Most very young puppies enjoy soft woolly toys that they can snuggle with and carry around. (You know they have outgrown them when they shred them up!) Avoid toys that have buttons, tabs or other enhancements that can be chewed off and swallowed. Soft toys that squeak are fun, but make sure your puppy does not disembowel the toy and remove (and swallow) the squeaker. Toys that rattle or make noise can excite a puppy, but they present the same danger as the squeaky kind and so require supervision. Hard rubber toys that bounce can also entertain a pup, but make sure that the toy is too big for your pup to swallow.

the same time, also watch for signs of intestinal distress. A call to your veterinarian might be in order to get his advice and be on the safe side.

An all-time favorite toy for puppies (young and old!) is the empty gallon milk jug. Hard plastic juice containers—46 ounces or more—are also excellent. Such containers make lots of noise when they are batted about, and puppies go crazy with delight as they play with them. However, they don't often last very long, so be sure to remove and replace them when they get chewed up.

A word of caution about homemade toys: be careful with your choices of non-traditional play objects. Never use old shoes or socks, since a puppy cannot distinguish between the old ones on which he's allowed to chew and the new ones in your closet that are strictly off-limits. That principle applies to anything that resembles something that you don't want your puppy to chew.

COLLARS

A lightweight nylon collar is the best choice for a very young pup. Quick-clip collars are easy to put on and remove, and they can be adjusted as the puppy grows. Introduce him to his collar as soon as he comes home to get him accustomed to wearing it. He'll get used to it quickly and won't mind a bit. Make sure that it is

COLLARING OUR CANINES

The standard flat collar with a buckle or a snap, in leather, nylon or cotton, is widely regarded as the everyday all-purpose collar. If the collar fits correctly, you should be able to fit two fingers between the collar and the dog's neck.

Leather Buckle Collars

Limited-Slip Collar

The martingale, Greyhound or limited-slip collar is preferred by many dog owners and trainers. It is fixed with an extra loop that tightens when pressure is applied to the leash. The martingale collar gets tighter but does not "choke" the dog. The limited-slip collar should only be used for walking and training, not for free play or interaction with another dog. These types of collar should never be left on the dog, as the extra loop can lead to accidents.

Choke collars, usually made of stainless steel, are made for training purposes, though are not recommended for small or heavily coated dogs, and certain other breeds, including the Welsh Terrier. Thin nylon choke leads are commonly used on show dogs while in the ring, though they are not practical for everyday use.

The harness, with two or three straps that attach over the dog's shoulders and around his torso, is a humane and safe alternative to the conventional collar. By and large, a well-made harness is virtually escape-proof. Harnesses are available in nylon and mesh and can be outfitted on most dogs, with chest girths ranging from 10 to 30 inches.

Snap Bolt Choke Collar

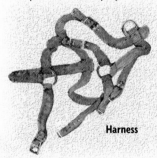

Harness

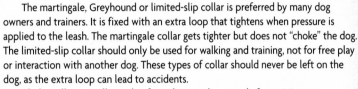

Nylon Collar

Quick-Click Closure

Snake Chain **Chrome Steel** **Fur-Saver**

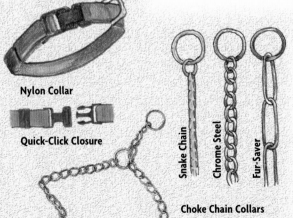

Choke Chain Collars

A head collar, composed of a nylon strap that goes around the dog's muzzle and a second strap that wraps around his neck, offers the owner better control over his dog. This device is recommended for problem-solving with dogs (including jumping up, pulling and aggressive behaviors), but must be used with care.

A training halter, including a flat collar and two straps, made of nylon and webbing, is designed for walking. There are several on the market; some are more difficult to put on the dog than others. The halter harness, with two small slip rings at each end, is recommended for ease of use.

This Welsh pup is becoming accustomed to his nylon lead, attached to a sturdy, light collar.

snug enough that it won't slip off, yet loose enough to be comfortable for the pup. You should be able to slip two fingers between the collar and his neck. Check the collar often, as puppies grow in spurts, and his collar can become too tight almost overnight.

Welsh puppies seldom object to any collar for more than a few minutes. The martingale collar (which is a double loop) prevents the dog from backing out as well as allowing you to make gentle corrections when he lunges ahead. It can be used for training as well. For the more athletic types, or those Welsh Terriers resistant to class instruction, a head collar is the answer. The head collar is an attention-getting device that allows you to turn the dog's head toward you, giving you better control over those persistent terrier distractions. Choke collars should never be used; the head

collar is more conducive to mutual understanding.

LEASHES

A 4-foot nylon lead is an excellent choice for a young puppy. It is lightweight and not as tempting to chew as a leather lead. For initial puppy walks and house-training purposes, the shorter 4-foot length will give you more control over the puppy. At first you don't want him wandering too far away from you and, when taking him out for toileting, you will want to keep him in the specific area chosen for his potty spot. As he becomes house-trained and polite on lead, you can progress to a 6-foot lead for walks.

The best lead for training is a 6-foot cotton lead. It is gentle on your hands and won't slip as easily as nylon. Welsh Terriers are generally cooperative about this "attachment for safety" program of ours. As an adult, when he won't be so likely to chew it to bits, your Welsh Terrier will look quite handsome with a matching leather collar and lead.

Once the puppy is heel-trained with a traditional leash, you can consider purchasing a retractable lead. This type of lead is excellent for walking adult dogs that are already leash-wise. The retractable lead allows the dog to roam farther away from you and explore a wider area when out walking, and also retracts when you need to keep him close.

HOME SAFETY FOR YOUR PUPPY

The importance of puppy-proofing cannot be overstated. In addition to making your house comfortable for your Welsh Terrier's arrival, you also must make sure that your house is safe for your puppy before you bring him home. There are countless hazards in the owner's personal living environment that a pup can sniff, chew, swallow or destroy. Many are obvious; others are not. Do a thorough advance house check to remove or rearrange those things that could hurt your puppy, keeping any potentially dangerous items out of areas to which he will have access.

Electrical cords are especially dangerous, since puppies view them as irresistible chew toys. Unplug and remove all exposed cords or fasten them beneath a baseboard where the puppy cannot reach them. Veterinarians and firefighters can tell you horror stories about electrical burns and house fires that resulted from puppy-chewed electrical cords. Consider this a most serious precaution for your puppy and the rest of your family.

Scout your home for tiny objects that might be seen at a pup's eye level. Keep medication bottles and cleaning supplies well out of reach, and do the same with waste baskets and other trash containers. It goes without saying that you should not use rodent poison or other toxic chemicals in any puppy area and that you must keep such containers safely locked up. You will be amazed at how many places a curious puppy can discover!

Once your house has cleared inspection, check your yard. A sturdy fence, well embedded into the ground, will give your dog a safe place to play and potty. Welsh Terriers are athletic dogs, so a 6-foot-high fence will be required to contain an agile youngster or adult. "Well-embedded into the ground" is especially important with terriers, who were born to dig. Check the fence periodically for necessary repairs. If there is a weak link or space to squeeze through or under, you can be sure a Welsh Terrier will discover it. A very determined pup may return to the same spot to "work on it" until he is able to get through.

TOXIC PLANTS

Plants are natural puppy magnets, but many can be harmful, even fatal, if ingested by a puppy or adult dog. Scout your yard and home interior and remove any plants, bushes or flowers that could be even mildly dangerous. It could save your puppy's life. You can obtain a complete list of toxic plants from your veterinarian, at the public library or by looking online.

A Dog-Safe Home

The dog-safety police are taking you and your new puppy on a house tour. Let's go room by room and see how safe your own home is for your new pup. The following items are doggie dangers, so either they must be removed or the dog should be monitored or not have access to these areas.

Living Room

- house plants (some varieties are poisonous)
- fireplace or wood-burning stove
- paint on the walls (lead-based paint is toxic)
- lead drapery weights (toxic lead)
- lamps and electrical cords
- carpet cleaners or deodorizers

Outdoor

- swimming pool
- pesticides
- toxic plants
- lawn fertilizers

Bathroom

- blue water in the toilet bowl
- medicine cabinet (filled with potentially deadly bottles)
- soap bars, bleach, drain cleaners, etc.
- tampons

Kitchen

- household cleaners in the kitchen cabinets
- glass jars and canisters
- sharp objects (like kitchen knives, scissors and forks)
- garbage can (with remnants of good-smelling things like onions, potato skins, apple or pear cores, peach pits, coffee beans, etc.)
- "people foods" that are toxic to dogs, like chocolate, raisins, grapes, nuts and onions

Garage

- antifreeze
- fertilizers (including rose foods)
- pesticides and rodenticides
- pool supplies (chlorine and other chemicals)
- oil and gasoline in containers
- sharp objects, electrical cords and power tools

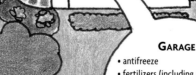

PUPPY PARASITES

Parasites are nasty little critters that live in or on your dog or puppy. Most puppies are born with ascarid roundworms, which are acquired from dormant ascarids residing in the dam. Other parasites can be acquired through contact with infected fecal matter. Take a stool sample to your vet for testing. He will prescribe a safe wormer to treat any parasites found in your puppy's stool. Always have a fecal test performed at your puppy's annual veterinary exam.

Also be very careful about doors that open into unfenced areas. Each family member must be on guard lest the Welsh Terrier slip out unnoticed.

The garage and shed can be hazardous places for a dog, as things like fertilizers, chemicals and tools are usually kept there. It's best to keep these areas off-limits to your Welsh. Antifreeze is especially dangerous to dogs, as they find the taste appealing and it takes only a few licks from the driveway to kill a dog, puppy or adult, small breed or large.

VISITING THE VETERINARIAN

A good veterinarian is your Welsh Terrier puppy's best health-insurance policy. If you do not already have a vet, ask friends and experienced dog people in your area for recommendations so that you can select a vet before you bring your Welsh Terrier puppy home. Also arrange for your puppy's first veterinary examination beforehand, since many vets do not have appointments available immediately and your puppy should visit the vet within a day or so of coming home.

It's important to make sure your puppy's first visit to the vet is a pleasant and positive one. The vet should take great care to befriend the pup and handle him gently to make their first meeting a positive experience. The vet will give the pup a thorough physical examination and set up a schedule for vaccinations and other necessary wellness visits. Be sure to show your vet any health and inoculation records, which you should have received from your breeder. Your vet is a great source of canine health information, so

Your Welsh Terrier puppy will be very curious about his new home and surroundings. Be sure that the yard is securely enclosed and that there are no dangerous plants or toxic chemicals in your landscaping.

be sure to ask questions and take notes. Creating a health journal for your puppy will make a handy reference for his wellness and any future health problems that may arise.

MEETING THE FAMILY

Your Welsh Terrier's homecoming is an exciting time for all members of the family, and it's only natural that everyone will be eager to meet him, pet him and play with him. However, for the puppy's sake, it's best to make these initial family meetings as uneventful as possible so that the pup is not overwhelmed with too much too soon. Remember, he has just left his dam and his littermates and is away from the breeder's home for the first time. Despite his fuzzy wagging tail, he is still apprehensive and wondering where he is and who all these strange humans are. It's best to let him explore on his own and meet the family members as he feels comfortable. Let him investigate all the new smells, sights and sounds at his own pace. Children should be especially careful to not get overly excited, use loud voices or hug the pup too tightly. Be calm, gentle and affectionate, and be ready to comfort him if he appears frightened or uneasy.

Be sure to show your puppy his new crate during this first day home. Toss a treat or two inside

> **THE WORRIES OF MANGE**
> Sometimes called "puppy mange," demodectic mange is passed to the puppy through the mother's milk. The microscopic mites that cause the condition take up residence in the puppy's hair follicles and sebaceous glands. Stress can cause the mites to multiply, causing bare patches on the face, neck and front legs. If neglected, it can lead to secondary bacterial infections, but if diagnosed and treated early, demodectic mange can be localized and controlled. Most pups recover without complications.

the crate; if he associates the crate with food, he will associate the crate with good things. Do not feed your puppy inside the crate, as this can lead to food-aggressive behavior. Leave the door ajar so he can wander in and out as he chooses.

FIRST NIGHT IN HIS NEW HOME

So much has happened in your Welsh Terrier puppy's first day away from the breeder. He's had his first car ride to his new home. He's met his new human family and perhaps the other family pets. He has explored his new house and yard, at least those places where he is to be allowed during his first weeks at home. He may have visited his new veterinarian. He has eaten his first meal or two away from his dam and littermates. Surely that's enough to tire out a nine-week-old Welsh Terrier pup...or so you hope!

It's bedtime. During the day, the pup investigated his crate, which is his new den and sleeping space, so it is not entirely strange to him. Line the crate with a soft towel or blanket that he can snuggle into and gently place him into the crate for the night. Some breeders send home a piece of bedding from where the pup slept with his littermates, and those familiar scents are a great comfort for the puppy on his first night without his siblings.

He will probably whine or cry. The puppy is objecting to the confinement and the fact that he is alone for the first time. This can be a stressful time for you as well as for the pup. It's important that you remain strong and don't let the puppy out of his crate to comfort him. He will fall asleep eventually. If you release him, the puppy will learn that crying means "out" and will continue that habit. You are laying the groundwork for future habits. Some breeders find that soft music can soothe a crying pup and help him get to sleep.

SOCIALIZING YOUR PUPPY
The first 20 weeks of your Welsh Terrier puppy's life are the most important of his entire lifetime. A properly socialized puppy will grow up to be a confident and

stable adult who will be a pleasure to live with and a welcome addition to the neighborhood.

The importance of socialization cannot be overemphasized. Research on canine behavior has proven that puppies who are not exposed to new sights, sounds, people and animals during their first 20 weeks of life will grow up to be timid and fearful, even aggressive, and unable to flourish outside of their home environment.

Socializing your puppy is not difficult and, in fact, will be a fun time for you both. Lead training goes hand in hand with socialization, so your puppy will be learning how to walk on a lead at the same time that he's meeting the neighborhood. Because the Welsh Terrier is such a terrific breed, everyone will enjoy meeting "the new kid on the block." Take him for short walks, to the park and to other dog-friendly places where he will encounter new people, especially children. Puppies automati-

Consider your pup's safety both indoors and out, by puppy-proofing and supervising. A pup doesn't know the difference between an electrical cord and a chew toy, which could lead to danger.

cally recognize children as "little people" and are drawn to play with them. Just make sure that you supervise these meetings and that the children do not get too rough or encourage him to play too hard. An overzealous pup can often nip too hard, frightening the child and in turn making the puppy overly excited. A bad experience in puppyhood can impact a dog for life, so a pup that has a negative experience with a child may grow up to be shy or even aggressive around children.

Take your puppy along on your daily errands. Puppies are

THE FAMILY FELINE

A resident cat has feline squatter's rights. The cat will treat the newcomer (your puppy) as she sees fit, regardless of what you do or say. So it's best to let the two of them work things out on their own terms. Cats have a height advantage and will generally leap to higher ground to avoid direct contact with a rambunctious pup. Some will hiss and boldly swat at a pup who passes by or tries to reach the cat. Keep the puppy under control in the presence of the cat and they will eventually become accustomed to each other.

Here's a hint: move the cat's litter box where the puppy can't get into it! It's best to do so well before the pup comes home so the cat is used to the new location.

natural "people magnets," and most people who see your pup will want to pet him. All of these encounters will help to mold him into a confident adult dog. Likewise, you will soon feel like a confident, responsible dog owner, rightly proud of your handsome Welsh Terrier.

Be especially careful of your puppy's encounters and experiences during the eight-to-ten-week-old period, which is also called the "fear period," if you have him for part of this time. This is a serious imprinting period, and all contact during this time should be gentle and positive. A frightening or negative event could leave a permanent impression that could affect his future behavior if a similar situation arises.

Also make sure that your puppy has received his first and second rounds of vaccinations before you expose him to other dogs or bring him to places that other dogs may frequent. Avoid dog parks and other strange-dog areas until your vet assures you that your puppy is fully immunized and resistant to the diseases that can be passed between canines. Discuss socialization with your breeder, as some breeders recommend socializing the puppy even before he has received all of his inoculations, depending on how outgoing the puppy may be.

LEADER OF THE PUPPY'S PACK

Like other canines, your puppy needs an authority figure, someone he can look up to and regard as the leader of his "pack." His first pack leader was his dam, who taught him to be polite and not chew too hard on her ears or nip at her muzzle. He learned those same lessons from his littermates. If he played too rough, they cried in pain and stopped the game, which sent an important message to the rowdy puppy.

As puppies play together, they are also struggling to determine who will be the boss. Being pack animals, dogs need someone to be in charge. If a litter of puppies remained together beyond puppyhood, one of the pups would emerge as the strongest one, the one who calls the shots.

Once your puppy leaves the pack, he will look intuitively for a new leader. If he does not recognize you as that leader, he will try to assume that position for himself. Of course, it is hard to imagine your adorable Welsh Terrier puppy trying to be in charge when he is so small and seemingly helpless. You must remember that these are natural canine instincts. Do not cave in and allow your pup to get the upper "paw"!

Just as socialization is so important during these first 20 weeks, so too is your puppy's early education. He was born without any bad habits. He does not know what is good or bad behavior. If he does things like nipping and digging, it's because he is having fun and doesn't know that humans consider these things as "bad." It's your job to teach him proper puppy manners, and this is the best time to accomplish that...before he has developed bad habits, since it is much more difficult to "unlearn" or correct unacceptable learned behavior than to teach good behavior from the start.

Make sure that all members of the family understand the importance of being consistent when training their new puppy. If you tell the puppy to stay off the sofa

Socialization begins at the breeder's home as the pups interact with their dam, their littermates and the people that live there.

and your daughter allows him to cuddle on the couch to watch her favorite television show, your pup will be confused about what he is and is not allowed to do. Have a family conference before your pup comes home so that everyone understands the basic principles of puppy training and the rules you have set forth for the pup, and agrees to follow them.

The old adage that "an ounce of prevention is worth a pound of cure" is especially true when it comes to puppies. It is much easier to prevent inappropriate behavior than it is to change it. It's also easier and less stressful for the pup, since it will keep discipline to a minimum and create a more positive learning environment for him. That, in turn, will also be easier on you!

CHEWING AND NIPPING

Nipping at fingers and toes is normal puppy behavior. Chewing is also the way that puppies investigate their surroundings. However, you will have to teach your puppy that chewing anything other than his toys is not acceptable. That won't happen overnight and at times puppy teeth will test your patience. However, if you allow nipping and chewing to continue, just think about the damage that a mature Welsh Terrier can do with a full set of adult terrier teeth.

Whenever your puppy nips your hand or fingers, cry out "Ouch!" in a loud voice, which should startle your puppy and stop him from nipping, even if only for a moment. Immediately distract him by offering a small treat or an appropriate toy for him to chew instead (which means having chew toys and puppy treats handy or in your pockets at all times). Praise him when he takes the toy and tell him what a good fellow he is. Praise is even more important in puppy training than discipline and correction.

Puppies also tend to nip at children more often than adults, since they perceive little ones to be more vulnerable and more similar to their littermates. Teach your children appropriate responses to nipping behavior. If they are unable to handle it themselves, you may have to intervene. Puppy nips can be quite painful

CONFINEMENT

It is wise to keep your puppy confined to a small "puppy-proofed" area of the house for his first few weeks at home. Gate or block off a space near the door he will use for outdoor potty trips. Expandable baby gates are useful to create puppy's designated area. If he is allowed to roam through the entire house or even only several rooms, it will be more difficult to house-train him.

and a child's frightened reaction will only encourage a puppy to nip harder, which is a natural canine response. As with all other puppy situations, interaction between your Welsh Terrier puppy and children should be supervised.

Chewing on objects, not just family members' fingers and ankles, is also normal canine behavior that can be especially tedious (for the owner, not the pup) during the teething period when the puppy's adult teeth are coming in. At this stage, chewing just plain feels good. Furniture legs and cabinet corners are common puppy favorites. Shoes and other personal items also taste pretty good to a pup.

The best solution is, once again, prevention. If you value something, keep it tucked away and out of reach. You can't hide your dining-room table in a closet, but you can try to deflect the chewing by applying a bitter product made just to deter dogs from chewing. Available in a spray or cream, this substance is vile-tasting, although safe for dogs, and most puppies will avoid the forbidden object after one tiny taste. You also can apply the product to your leather leash if the puppy tries to chew on his lead during leash-training sessions.

Keep a ready supply of safe chews handy to offer your Welsh Terrier as a distraction when he starts to chew on something that's a "no-no." Remember, at this tender age he does not yet know what is permitted or forbidden, so you have to be "on call" every minute he's awake and on the prowl.

You may lose a treasure or two during puppy's growing-up period, and the furniture could sustain a nasty nick or two. These can be trying times, so be prepared for those inevitable accidents and comfort yourself in knowing that this too shall pass.

Adding a Welsh Terrier to your household means adding a new family member who will need your care each and every day. When your Welsh Terrier pup first comes home, you will start a routine with him so that, as he grows up, your dog will have a daily schedule just as you do. The aspects of your dog's daily care will likewise become regular parts of your day, so you'll both have a new schedule. Dogs learn by consistency and thrive on routine: regular times for meals, exercise, grooming and potty trips are just as important for your dog as they are to you! Your dog's schedule will depend much on your family's daily routine, but remember that you now have a new member of the family who is part of your day every day.

FEEDING

Feeding your dog the best diet is based on various factors, including age, activity level, overall condition and size of breed. When you visit the breeder, he will share with you his advice about the proper diet for your dog based on his experience with the breed and the foods with which he has had success. Likewise, your vet will be a helpful source of advice throughout the dog's life and will aid you in planning a diet for optimal health.

FEEDING THE PUPPY

Of course, your pup's very first food will be his dam's milk. There may be special situations

---

NOT HUNGRY?

No dog in his right mind would turn down his dinner, would he? If you notice that your dog has lost interest in his food, there could be any number of causes. Dental problems are a common cause of appetite loss, one that is often overlooked. If your dog has a toothache, a loose tooth or sore gums from infection, chances are it doesn't feel so good to chew. Think about when you've had a toothache! If your dog does not approach the food bowl with his usual enthusiasm, look inside his mouth for signs of a problem. Whatever the cause, you'll want to consult your vet so that your chow hound can get back to his happy, hungry self as soon as possible.

in which pups fail to nurse, necessitating that the breeder hand-feed them with a formula, but for the most part pups spend the first weeks of life nursing from their dam. The breeder weans the pups by gradually introducing solid foods and decreasing the milk meals. Pups may even start themselves off on the weaning process, albeit inadvertently, if they snatch bites from their mom's food bowl.

By the time the pups are ready for new homes, they are fully weaned and eating a good puppy food. As a new owner, you may be thinking, "Great! The breeder has taken care of the hard part." Not so fast.

A puppy's first year of life is the time when all or most of his growth and development takes place. This is a delicate time, and diet plays a huge role in proper skeletal and muscular formation. Improper diet and exercise habits can lead to damaging problems that will compromise the dog's health and movement for his entire life. That being said, new owners should not worry needlessly. With the myriad types of food formulated specifically for growing pups of different-sized breeds, dog-food manufacturers have taken much of the guesswork out of feeding your puppy well. Since growth-food formulas are designed to provide the nutrition that a growing puppy needs, it is

Ch. Vicway Modesty Blaise is a perfect example of a well-maintained Welsh Terrier in top condition. Diet, exercise and grooming are important parts of the dog's care and overall well-being.

unnecessary and, in fact, can prove harmful to add supplements to the diet. Research has shown that too much of certain vitamin supplements and minerals predispose a dog to skeletal problems. It's by no means a case of "if a little is good, a lot is better." At every stage of your dog's life, too much or too little in the way of nutrients can be harmful, which is why a manufactured complete food is the easiest way to know that your dog is getting what he needs.

Because of a young pup's small body and accordingly small digestive system, his daily portion will be divided up into small meals throughout the day. This can mean starting off with three or more meals a day and decreasing the number of meals as the pup matures. Eventually you can feed only one meal a day, although it is generally thought that dividing the day's food into two meals on a morning/evening schedule is healthier for the dog's digestion.

Regarding the feeding schedule, feeding the pup at the same times and in the same place each day is important for both house-breaking purposes and establishing the dog's everyday routine. As for the amount to feed, growing puppies generally need proportionately more food per body weight than their adult counterparts, but a pup should never be allowed to gain excess weight. Dogs of all ages should be kept in proper body condition, but extra weight can strain a pup's developing frame, causing skeletal problems.

Watch your pup's weight as he grows and, if the recommended amounts seem to be too much or too little for your pup, consult the vet about appropriate dietary changes. Keep in mind that treats, although small, can quickly add up throughout the day, contributing unnecessary calories. Treats are fine when used prudently; opt for dog treats specially formulated to be healthy or for nutritious snacks like small pieces of cheese or cooked chicken.

FEEDING THE ADULT DOG

For the adult (meaning physically mature) dog, feeding properly is about maintenance, not growth. Again, correct weight is a concern. Your dog should appear fit and should have an evident "waist." His ribs should not be protruding (a sign of being underweight), but they should be covered by only a slight layer of

SWITCHING FOODS

There are certain times in a dog's life when it becomes necessary to switch his food; for example, from puppy to adult food and then from adult to senior-dog food. Additionally, you may decide to feed your pup a different type of food from what he received from the breeder, and there may be "emergency" situations in which you can't find your dog's normal brand and have to offer something else temporarily. Anytime a change is made, for whatever reason, the switch must be done gradually. You don't want to upset the dog's stomach or end up with a picky eater who refuses to eat something new. A tried-and-true approach is, over the course of about a week, to mix a little of the new food in with the old, increasing the proportion of new to old as the days progress. At the end of the week, you'll be feeding his regular portions of the new food, and he will barely notice the change.

fat. Under normal circumstances, an adult dog can be maintained fairly easily with a high-quality nutritionally complete adult-formula food.

Factor treats into your dog's overall daily caloric intake, and avoid offering table scraps. Not only are certain "people foods," like chocolate, onions, grapes, raisins and nuts, toxic to dogs, but feeding from the table encourages begging and overeating. Over-weight dogs are more prone to health problems. Research has even shown that obesity takes years off a dog's life. With that in mind, resist the urge to overfeed and over-treat. Don't make unnecessary additions to your dog's diet, whether with tidbits or with extra vitamins and minerals.

The amount of food needed for proper maintenance will vary depending on the individual dog's activity level, but you will be able to tell whether the daily portions are keeping him in good shape. With the wide variety of good complete foods available, choosing what to feed is largely a matter of personal preference. Just as with the puppy, the adult dog should have consistency in his mealtimes and feeding place. In addition to a consistent routine, regular mealtimes also allow the owner to see how much his dog is eating. If the dog seems never to be satisfied or, likewise, becomes uninterested in his food, the

DIET DON'TS
- Got milk? Don't give it to your dog! Dogs cannot tolerate large quantities of cows' milk, as they do not have the enzymes to digest lactose.
- You may have heard of dog owners' who add raw eggs to their dogs' food for a shiny coat or to make the food more palatable, but consumption of raw eggs too often can cause a deficiency of the vitamin biotin.
- Avoid feeding table scraps, as they will upset the balance of the dog's complete food. Additionally, fatty or highly seasoned foods can cause upset canine stomachs.
- Do not offer raw meat to your dog. Raw meat can contain parasites; it also is high in fat.
- Vitamin A toxicity in dogs can be caused by too much raw liver, especially if the dog already gets enough vitamin A in his balanced diet, which should be the case.
- Bones like chicken, pork chop and other soft bones are not suitable, as they easily splinter.

Welsh Terriers are enthusiastic "chow hounds" who approach mealtimes with vigor!

owner will know right away that something is wrong and can consult the vet.

DIETS FOR THE AGING DOG

A good rule of thumb is that once a dog has reached 75% of his expected lifespan, he has reached "senior citizen" or geriatric status. Your Welsh Terrier will be considered a senior at about 8 or 9 years of age; he has a projected lifespan of at least 12 years. Terriers in general are relatively long-lived dogs.

What does aging have to do with your dog's diet? No, he won't get a discount at the local diner's early-bird special. Yes, he will require some dietary changes to accommodate the changes that come along with increased age. One change is that the older dog's dietary needs become more similar to that of a puppy. Specifically, dogs can metabolize more protein as youngsters and seniors than in the adult-maintenance stage. Discuss with your vet whether you need to switch to a higher-protein or senior-formulated food or whether your current adult-dog food contains sufficient nutrition for the senior.

Watching the dog's weight remains essential, even more so in the senior stage. Older dogs are already more vulnerable to illness, and obesity only contributes to their susceptibility to problems. As the older dog becomes less active and thus exercises less, his regular portions may cause him to gain weight. At this point, you may consider decreasing his daily food intake or switching to a reduced-calorie food. As with other changes, you should consult your vet for advice.

DON'T FORGET THE WATER!

For a dog, it's always time for a drink! Regardless of what type of food he eats, there's no doubt that he needs plenty of water. Fresh cold water, in a clean bowl, should be freely available to your dog at all times. There are special circumstances, such as during puppy housebreaking, when you will want to monitor your pup's water intake so that you will be able to predict when he will need to relieve himself, but water must be available to him nonetheless.

Water is essential for hydration and proper body function just as it is in humans.

You will get to know how much your dog typically drinks in a day. Of course, in the heat or if exercising vigorously, he will be more thirsty and will drink more. However, if he begins to drink noticeably more water for no apparent reason, this could signal any of various problems, and you are advised to consult your vet.

Water is the best drink for dogs. Some owners are tempted to give milk from time to time or to moisten dry food with milk, but dogs do not have the enzymes necessary to digest the lactose in milk, which is much different from the milk that nursing puppies receive. Therefore, stick with clean fresh water to quench your dog's thirst, and always have it readily available to him.

A water bowl should be kept outside so that your Welsh can quench his thirst during outdoor play and exercise.

PUPPY STEPS

Puppies are brimming with activity and enthusiasm. It seems that they can play all day and night without tiring, but don't overdo your puppy's exercise regimen. Easy does it for the puppy's first six to nine months. Keep walks brief and don't let the puppy engage in stressful jumping games. The puppy frame is delicate, and too much exercise during those critical growing months can cause injury to his bone structure, ligaments and musculature. Save his first jog for his first birthday!

EXERCISE

The Welsh Terrier, like all other terrier breeds, is an active dog that welcomes the chance to exercise. Two vigorous walks daily are ideal for the adult Welsh. Do not begin brisk walks with your Welsh until he is at least four months of age. As the dog reaches adulthood, the speed and distance of the walks can be increased as long as they are both kept reasonable and comfortable for both of you. A good walk will stimulate the youngster's heart rate as well as promote development of musculature.

Most importantly, your Welsh Terrier looks for structured time to spend with his owner in an active

A Welsh's body should appear fit and athletic.

suddenly over-exercised; instead, he should be encouraged to increase exercise slowly. Also remember that not only is exercise essential to keep the dog's body fit but it also is essential to his mental well-being. A bored dog will find something to do, which often manifests itself in some type of destructive behavior. In this sense, exercise is essential for the owner's mental well-being as well!

GROOMING

COAT CARE

The Welsh Terrier has a wiry outer coat and a soft, somewhat woolly, undercoat. Neither one actually casts out or sheds; that is, the hair does not reach a certain stage of growth and fall out in profusion all over the furniture. Dead hairs are adequately removed with a good weekly brushing and combing. If the coat is not properly trimmed, the adorable puppy will become a shaggy, unattractive woolly-bully within a year, with matted lumps harboring unwanted parasites.

pursuit of fun. Play sessions and letting the dog run free in the fenced yard also are great exercise for the Welsh Terrier. Keep an eye on your Welsh's yard time to make sure he's staying safe and out of mischief. Fetching games can be played indoors or out; these are excellent for giving your dog active play that he will enjoy. Chasing things that move comes naturally to dogs of all breeds, and the Welsh has strong instincts for catching things on the run. If you choose to play games outdoors, you must have a securely fenced-in yard and/or have the dog attached to at least a 25-foot light line for security. You want your Welsh Terrier to run, but not run away!

Bear in mind that an overweight dog should never be

Don't expect a Welsh Terrier puppy to cooperate with being groomed for more than five or ten minutes. Begin with short daily sessions and lengthen them as the puppy learns to tolerate the brushing and handling. A worthwhile investment is a small

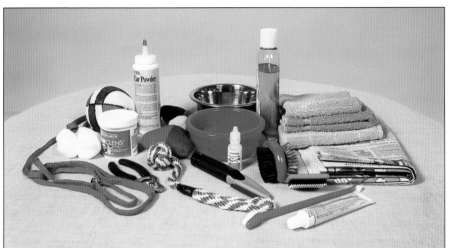

Ask your breeder for advice about what type of equipment you'll need to care for your terrier's wiry coat.

fold-up grooming table with an adjustable noose at one end to keep the dog's head up and facing the right direction. You'll get good use out of it for 12 to 14 years. It's important that the dog feel perfectly safe, so if you use something else, such as an ordinary table, for grooming, be sure it is steady and has a non-slip surface. Never leave any dog—puppy or adult—unsupervised on the table. A fall could cause serious injury.

The only grooming required for the first few weeks is gentle brushing and combing, because the primary purpose is to accustom your puppy to being handled for the real grooming to come. A thorough brushing and combing will precede every trimming session.

There are two ways to keep the Welsh looking as neat and

WATER SHORTAGE

No matter how well behaved your dog is, bathing is always a project! Nothing can substitute for a good warm bath, but owners do have the option of giving their dogs "dry" baths. Pet shops sell excellent products, in both powder and spray forms, designed for spot-cleaning your dog. These dry shampoos are convenient for touch-up jobs when you don't have the time to bathe your dog in the traditional way.

Muddy feet, messy behinds and smelly coats can be spot-cleaned and deodorized with a "wet-nap"-style cleaner. On those days when your dog insists on rolling in fresh goose droppings and there's no time for a bath, a spot bath can save the day. These pre-moistened wipes are also handy for other grooming needs like wiping faces, ears and eyes and freshening tails and behinds.

handsome as he should. The preferred method is called plucking, or stripping, and for anyone not familiar with the process, it is best undertaken with the instruction of someone who knows exactly how to do it and can show you. It is not difficult, but it is time-consuming. Done correctly, stripping will not hurt the dog. A few hairs at a time are methodically lifted and pulled (in the direction the hair grows) using the fingers or a stripping knife.

All of the trimming is done to follow the lines of the dog. The Welsh Terrier has no frills or skirts or other enhancements to his outline. Short eyebrows are left to protect his small, deep-set eyes from nettles and twigs. All hair on the inside of the ears is removed so they fold properly for protection and are more easily kept clean. The only parts left somewhat long are the furnishings, or whiskers, on the muzzle and on the legs, and that's in part because they can take months to grow back in. The front legs are trimmed as columns, the face is styled as a rectangle and the hindquarters furnishings follow the angulation. Use photographs of show dogs for guidance.

Billy poses on a grooming table. The lead is attached overhead to the table's metal arm.

The alternative method is to use an electric clipper, following the same pattern. A few lessons in "clipper control" would be a good idea, since it is only easy when you've got the hang of it. Holding a noisy machine in one hand and getting the Welsh to stand still when you put this object on his head is not as easy at it looks when watching a long-time terrierman or other professional! Clipping is quicker, but it has a downside. When the hairs of both coats (wire and soft) are cut, rather than just dead hair removed, the coat often loses its deep color. Plucking or stripping allows the strong-colored tips of new hairs to be seen.

Of course, there is a third method—that is to pack your Welsh into the car, head to a professional groomer and pay to have someone else do it, either by stripping or clipping. No matter which method you choose, this coat work only needs to be undertaken about every three months.

For weekly grooming, you'll need two brushes. One is a terrier palm pad (also called a dolling-up pad) and the other a slicker (made with bent wires) or a stiff bristle brush. The pad is used on the furnishings, brushing against and then with the way the hair grows. The slicker or bristle brush is used on the rest of the dog. Use both gently, getting down to the skin, but not digging

into it. You'll need a metal comb and a pair of scissors for trimming between the pads of the feet and around the edges of the feet, ears and so on.

All of this brushing promotes good healthy skin and removes dead hair as well as dirt and debris caught in the coat. It will also leave you with a Welsh

The palm pad is used on the furnishings, both against and with the lie of the hair.

The slicker brush is used to thoroughly brush the rest of the body.

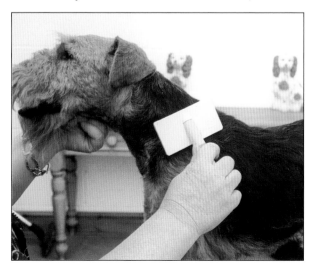

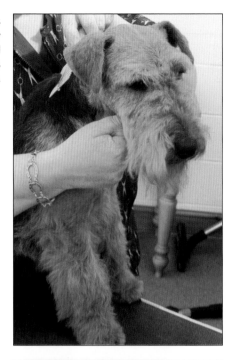

A metal comb is helpful for detangling and removing debris from the coat.

The excess hair growing on the bottom of the feet, between the pads, should be carefully scissored.

Terrier that is handsome to look at and nice to have around the house.

Many Welsh Terriers are bathed only two or three times in their lives. Their coats shed dirt and with it any doggy odor. Most Welsh Terriers love the rain, which is a good thing, considering their country of origin, but after coming in from the rain, a good toweling and a brushing are all that's needed. The wire Welsh coat is akin to a duck's back! However, if your dog has rolled in muck or mud, a bath will be in order. Use a dog shampoo (people shampoos contain ingredients harmful to the dog's skin and coat) and rinse thoroughly several times. Muddy paws, and face furnishings caught up in the dinner dish, only need rinsing off as needed. Towel-dry, brush and comb all hair into place.

NAIL CLIPPING

Having his nails trimmed is not on many dogs' lists of favorite things to do. With this in mind, you will need to accustom your puppy to the procedure at a young age so that he will sit still (well, as still as he can) for his pedicures. Long nails can cause the dog's feet to spread, which is not good for him; likewise, long nails can hurt if they unintentionally scratch, not good for you!

Some dogs' nails are worn down naturally by regular walking on hard surfaces, so the frequency with which you clip depends on your individual dog. Look at his nails from time to time and clip as needed; a good way to know when it's time for a trim is if you hear your dog clicking as he walks across the floor.

There are several types of nail clippers and even electric nail-grinding tools made for dogs; first we'll discuss using the clipper. To start, have your clipper ready and some doggie treats on

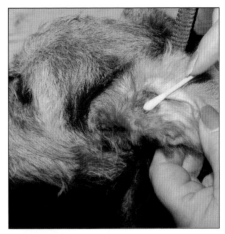

Never probe into the ear with a cotton swab; only clean that which is visible. It is safer to use a soft cotton wipe. Ear cleanser for dogs is available at pet shops or through your vet.

THE EARS KNOW

Examining and cleaning your puppy's ears helps ensure good internal health. The ears are the eyes to the dog's innards! Begin handling your puppy's ears when he's still young so that he doesn't protest every time you lift a flap or touch his ears. Yeast and bacteria are two of the culprits that you can detect by examining the ear. You will notice a strong, often foul, odor, debris, redness or some kind of discharge. All of these point to health problems that can worsen over time. Additionally, you are on the lookout for wax accumulation, ear mites and other tiny bothersome parasites and their even tinier droppings. You may have to pluck hair with tweezers in order to have a better view into the dog's ears, but this is painless if done carefully. Healthy ears should be gently cleaned once a week, using an ear-cleaning formula and a soft wipe or pad.

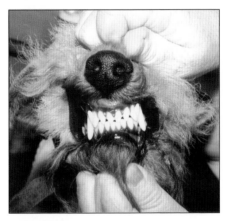

Check your dog's teeth regularly to ensure that plaque is not accumulating on the teeth and gums.

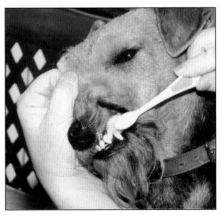

Initiate a home dental-care regimen. Use toothbrushes and toothpaste made especially for dogs.

you do not want to cut into the quick. On that note, if you do cut the quick, which will cause bleeding, you can stem the flow of blood with a styptic pencil or other clotting agent. If you mistakenly nip the quick, do not panic or fuss, as this will cause the pup to be afraid. Simply reassure the pup, stop the bleeding and move on to the next nail. Don't be

You will appreciate the time you spent acclimating the pup to his pedicures when you have a politely behaved adult who stands still while you clip.

hand. You want your pup to view his nail-clipping sessions in a positive light, and what better way to convince him than with food? You may want to enlist the help of an assistant to comfort the pup and offer treats as you concentrate on the clipping itself. The guillotine-type clipper is thought of by many as the easiest type to use; the nail tip is inserted into the opening, and blades on the top and bottom snip it off in one clip.

Start by grasping the pup's paw; a little pressure on the foot pad causes the nail to extend, making it easier to clip. Clip off a little at a time. If you can see the "quick," which is a blood vessel that runs through each nail, you will know how much to trim, as

SCOOTING HIS BOTTOM

Here's a doggy problem that many owners tend to neglect. If your dog is scooting his rear end around the carpet, he probably is experiencing anal-sac impaction or blockage. The anal sacs are the two grape-sized glands on either side of the dog's vent. The dog cannot empty these glands, which become filled with a foul-smelling material. The dog may attempt to lick the area to relieve the pressure. He may also rub his anus on your walls, furniture or floors.

Don't neglect your dog's rear end during grooming sessions. By squeezing both sides of the anus with a soft cloth, you can express some of the material in the sacs. If the material is pasty and thick, you likely will need the assistance of a veterinarian. Vets know how to express the glands and can show you how to do it correctly without hurting the dog or spraying yourself with the contents.

discouraged; you will become a professional canine pedicurist with practice.

You may or may not be able to see the quick, so it's best to just clip off a small bit at a time. If you see a dark dot in the center of the nail, this is the quick and your cue to stop clipping. Tell the puppy he's a "good boy" and offer a piece of treat with each nail. You can also use nail-clipping time to examine the foot-pads, making sure that they are not dry and cracked and that nothing has become embedded in them.

The nail grinder, the other choice, is many owners' first choice. Accustoming the puppy to the sound of the grinder and sensation of the buzz presents fewer challenges than the clipper, and there's no chance of cutting through the quick. Use the grinder on a low setting and always talk soothingly to your dog. He won't mind his salon visit, and he'll have nicely polished nails as well.

EYE CARE

During grooming sessions, pay extra attention to the condition of your dog's eyes. If the area around the eyes is soiled or if tear staining has occurred, there are various cleaning agents made especially for this purpose. Look at the dog's eyes to make sure no debris has entered; dogs with large eyes and those who spend time outdoors are especially prone to this.

The signs of an eye infection are obvious: mucus, redness, puffiness, scabs or other signs of irritation. If your dog's eyes become infected, the vet will likely prescribe an antibiotic ointment for treatment. If you notice signs of more serious problems, such as opacities in the eye, which usually indicate cataracts, consult the vet at once. Taking time to pay attention to your dog's eyes will alert you in the early stages of any problem so that you can get your dog treatment as soon as possible. You could save your dog's sight!

ID FOR YOUR DOG

You love your Welsh Terrier and want to keep him safe. Of course,

PET OR STRAY?

Besides the obvious benefit of providing your contact information to whoever finds your lost dog, an ID tag makes your dog more approachable and more likely to be recovered. A strange dog wandering the neighborhood without a collar and tags will look like a stray, while the collar and tags indicate that the dog is someone's pet. Even if the ID tags become detached from the collar, the collar alone will make a person more likely to pick up the dog.

you take every precaution to prevent his escaping from the yard or becoming lost or stolen. You have a sturdy high fence and you always keep your dog on-lead when out and about in public places. If your dog is not properly identified, however, you are over-looking a major aspect of his safety. We hope to never be in a situation where our dog is miss-ing, but we should practice prevention in the unfortunate case that this happens; identification greatly increases the chances of your dog's being returned to you

There are several ways to identify your dog. First, the tradi-tional dog tag should be a staple in your dog's wardrobe, attached

In a crate is the safest way for your Welsh to travel.

CAR CAUTION
You may like to bring your canine companion along on the daily errands, but if you will be running in and out from place to place and can't bring him indoors with you, leave him at home. Your dog should never be left alone in the car, not even for a minute—never! A car heats up very quickly, and even a cracked-open window will not help. In fact, leaving the window cracked will be dangerous if the dog becomes uncomfortable and tries to escape. When in doubt, leave your dog home, where you know he will be safe.

to his everyday collar. Tags can be made of sturdy plastic and various metals and should include your contact information so that a person who finds the dog can get in touch with you right away to arrange his return. Many people today enjoy the wide range of decorative tags available, so have fun and create a tag to match your dog's personality. Of course, it is important that the tag stays on the collar, so have a secure "O" ring attachment; you also can explore the type of tag that slides right onto the collar.

In addition to the ID tag, which every dog should wear even if identified by another method, two other forms of identi-fication have become popular: microchipping and tattooing. In microchipping, a tiny scannable chip is painlessly inserted under the dog's skin. The number is registered to you so that, if your lost dog turns up at a clinic or shelter, the chip can be scanned to retrieve your contact information.

The advantage of the microchip is that it is a permanent form of ID, but there are some factors to consider. Several different companies make microchips, and not all are compatible with the others' scanning devices. It's best to find a company with a universal microchip that can be read by scanners made by other companies as well. It won't do any good to have the dog chipped if the information cannot be retrieved. Also, not every humane society, shelter and clinic is equipped with a scanner, although more and more facilities are equipping themselves. In fact, many shelters microchip dogs that they adopt out to new homes.

Because the microchip is not visible to the eye, the dog must wear a tag that states that he is microchipped so that whoever picks him up will know to have him scanned. He of course also should have a tag with contact information in case his chip cannot be read. Humane societies and veterinary clinics offer microchipping service, which is usually very affordable.

Though less popular than microchipping, tattooing is

another permanent method of ID for dogs. Most vets perform this service, and there are also clinics that perform dog tattooing. This is also an affordable procedure and one that will not cause much discomfort for the dog. It is best to put the tattoo in a visible area, such as the ear, to deter theft. It is sad to say that there are cases of dogs' being stolen and sold to research laboratories, but such laboratories will not accept tattooed dogs.

To ensure that the tattoo is effective in aiding your dog's return to you, the tattoo number must be registered with a national organization. That way, when someone finds a tattooed dog, a phone call to the registry will quickly match the dog with his owner.

Your Welsh Terrier's ID tag must be securely fastened to his everyday collar.

BASIC TRAINING PRINCIPLES: PUPPY VS. ADULT

There's a big difference between training an adult dog and training a young puppy. With a young puppy, everything is new. When your pup comes home with you, he will be experiencing many things, and he has nothing with which to compare these experiences. Up to this point, he has been with his dam and littermates, not one-on-one with people except in his interactions with his breeder and visitors to the litter.

When you first bring the puppy home, he is eager to please you. This means that he accepts doing things your way. During the next couple of months, he will absorb the basis of everything he needs to know for the rest of his life. This early age is even referred to as the "sponge" stage. After that, for the next 18 months, it's up to you to reinforce good manners by building on the foundation that you've established. Once your puppy is reliable in basic commands and behavior and has reached the appropriate age, you may gradually introduce him to some of the interesting sports, games and activities available to pet owners and their dogs.

Raising your puppy is a family affair. Each member of the family

> ### LEADER OF THE PACK
> Canines are pack animals. They live according to pack rules, and every pack has only one leader. Guess what? That's you! To establish your position of authority, lay down the rules and be fair and good-natured in all your dealings with your dog. He will consider young children as his littermates, but the one who trains him, who feeds him, who grooms him, who expects him to come into line, that's his leader. And he who leads must be obeyed.

must know what rules to set forth for the puppy and how to use the same one-word commands to mean exactly the same thing every time. Even if yours is a large family, one person will soon be considered by the pup to be the leader, the Alpha person in his pack, the "boss" who must be obeyed. Often that highly regarded person turns out to be the one who feeds the puppy. Food ranks very high on the puppy's list of important things! That's why your puppy is rewarded with small treats along with verbal praise when he responds to you correctly. As the puppy learns to do what you want him to do, the food rewards are

OUR CANINE KIDS

"Everything I learned about parenting, I learned from my dog." How often adults recognize that their parenting skills are mere extensions of the education they acquired while caring for their dogs. Many owners refer to their dogs as their "kids" and treat their canine companions like real members of the family. Surveys indicate that a majority of dog owners talk to their dogs regularly, celebrate their dogs' birthdays and purchase Christmas gifts for their dogs. Another survey shows that dog owners take their dogs to the veterinarian more frequently than they visit their own physicians.

gradually eliminated and only the praise remains. If you were to keep up with the food treats, you could have two problems on your hands—an obese dog and a beggar.

Training begins the minute your Welsh Terrier puppy steps through the doorway of your home, so don't make the mistake of putting the puppy on the floor and telling him by your actions to "Go for it! Run wild!" Even if this is your first puppy, you must act as if you know what you're doing: be the boss. An uncertain pup may be terrified to move, while a bold one will be ready to take you at your word and start plotting to destroy the house! Before you collected your puppy, you decided where his own special

Everyone in the family should take part in the Welsh Terrier's training so that the dog will respect and obey all members of his "pack."

Welsh Terriers on a winter walk in Finland with Jaana Matto.

Working with a professional trainer will speed up your progress with an adopted adult dog. You'll need patience, too. Some new rules may be close to impossible for the dog to accept. After all, he's been successful so far by doing everything his way! (Patience again.) He may agree with your instruction for a few days and then slip back into his old ways, so you must be just as consistent and understanding in your teaching as you would be with a puppy. (More patience needed yet again!) Your dog has to learn to pay attention to your voice, your family, the daily routine, new smells, new sounds and, in some cases, even a new climate.

One of the most important things to find out about a newly

place would be, and that's where to put him when you first arrive home. Give him a house tour after he has investigated his area and had a nap and a bathroom "pit stop."

It's worth mentioning here that if you've adopted an adult dog that is completely trained to your liking, lucky you! You're off the hook! However, if that dog spent his life up to this point in a kennel, or even in a good home but without any real training, be prepared to tackle the job ahead. A dog three years of age or older with no previous training cannot be blamed for not knowing what he was never taught. While the dog is trying to understand and learn your rules, at the same time he has to unlearn many of his previously self-taught habits and general view of the world.

BASIC PRINCIPLES OF DOG TRAINING

1. Start training early. A young puppy is ready, willing and able.
2. Timing is your all-important tool. Praise at the exact time that the dog responds correctly. Pay close attention.
3. Patience is almost as important as timing!
4. Repeat! The same word has to mean the same thing every time.
5. In the beginning, praise all correct behavior verbally, along with treats and petting.

adopted adult dog is his reaction to children (yours and others), strangers and your friends, and how he acts upon meeting other dogs. If he was not socialized with dogs as a puppy, this could be a major problem. This does not mean that he's a "bad" dog, a vicious dog or an aggressive dog; rather, it means that he has no idea how to read another dog's body language. There's no way for him to tell whether the other dog is a friend or foe. Survival instinct takes over, telling him to attack first and ask questions later. This definitely calls for professional help and, even then, may not be a behavior that can be corrected 100% reliably (or even at all). If you have a puppy, this is why it is so very important to introduce your young puppy properly to other puppies and "dog-friendly" adult dogs.

HOUSE-TRAINING YOUR WELSH TERRIER

Dogs are tactility-oriented when it comes to house-training. In other words, they respond to the surface on which they are given approval to eliminate. The choice is yours (the dog's version is in parentheses): The lawn (including the neighbors' lawns)? A bare patch of earth under a tree (where people like to sit and relax in the summertime)? Concrete steps or patio (all sidewalks, garages and basement floors)? The curbside (watch out for cars)? A small area of crushed stone in a corner of the yard (mine!)? The latter is the best choice if you can manage it, because it will remain strictly for the dog's use and is easy to keep clean.

You can start out with paper-training indoors and switch over to an outdoor surface as the puppy matures and gains control over his need to eliminate. For the nay-sayers, don't worry—this won't mean that the dog will soil on every piece of newspaper lying around the house. You are training him to go outside, remember? Starting out by paper-training often is the only choice for a city dog.

WHEN YOUR PUPPY'S "GOT TO GO"
Your puppy's need to relieve himself is seemingly non-stop, but signs of improvement will be seen each week. From 9 to 10

Your pup's mealtimes have a direct effect on the house-training schedule. What goes in must come out; with a pup, that's usually sooner, not later!

A fenced yard makes the task of house-training much easier, but the pup must learn the difference between potty time and exploring time.

period. If you can't get home in the middle of the day, plan to hire a dog-sitter or ask a neighbor to come over to take the pup outside, feed him his lunch and then take him out again about ten or so minutes after he's eaten. Also make arrangements with that or another person to be your "emergency" contact if you have to stay late on the job. Remind yourself—repeatedly—that this hectic schedule improves as the puppy gets older.

HOME WITHIN A HOME

Your Welsh Terrier puppy needs to be confined to one secure, puppy-proof area when no one is able to watch his every move. Generally, the kitchen is the place

weeks old, the puppy will have to be taken outside every time he wakes up, about 10–15 minutes after every meal and after every period of play—all day long, from first thing in the morning until his bedtime! That's a total of ten or more trips per day to teach the puppy where it's okay to relieve himself. With that schedule in mind, you can see that house-training a young puppy is not a part-time job. It requires someone to be home all day.

If that seems overwhelming or impossible, do a little planning. For example, plan to pick up your puppy at the start of a vacation

DAILY SCHEDULE

How many relief trips does your puppy need per day? A puppy up to the age of 14 weeks will need to go outside about 8 to 12 times per day! You will have to take the pup out any time he starts sniffing around the floor or turning in small circles, as well as after naps, meals, games and lessons or whenever he's released from his crate. Once the puppy is 14 to 22 weeks of age, he will require only 6 to 8 relief trips. At the ages of 22 to 32 weeks, the puppy will require about 5 to 7 trips. Adult dogs typically require 4 relief trips per day, in the morning, afternoon, evening and late at night.

CANINE DEVELOPMENT SCHEDULE

It is important to understand how and at what age a puppy develops into adulthood. If you are a puppy owner, consult the following Canine Development Schedule to determine the stage of development your puppy is currently experiencing. This knowledge will help you as you work with the puppy in the weeks and months ahead.

PERIOD	AGE	CHARACTERISTICS
FIRST TO THIRD	BIRTH TO SEVEN WEEKS	Puppy needs food, sleep and warmth and responds to simple and gentle touching. Needs mother for security and disciplining. Needs littermates for learning and interacting with other dogs. Pup learns to function within a pack and learns pack order of dominance. Begin socializing pup with adults and children for short periods. Pup begins to become aware of his environment.
FOURTH	EIGHT TO TWELVE WEEKS	Brain is fully developed. Pup needs socializing with outside world. Remove from mother and littermates. Needs to change from canine pack to human pack. Human dominance necessary. Fear period occurs between 8 and 10 weeks. Avoid fright and pain.
FIFTH	THIRTEEN TO SIXTEEN WEEKS	Training and formal obedience should begin. Less association with other dogs, more with people, places, situations. Period will pass easily if you remember this is pup's change-to-adolescence time. Be firm and fair. Flight instinct prominent. Permissiveness and over-disciplining can do permanent damage. Praise for good behavior.
JUVENILE	FOUR TO EIGHT MONTHS	Another fear period about 7 to 8 months of age. It passes quickly, but be cautious of fright and pain. Sexual maturity reached. Dominant traits established. Dog should understand sit, down, come and stay by now.

NOTE: THESE ARE APPROXIMATE TIME FRAMES. ALLOW FOR INDIVIDUAL DIFFERENCES IN PUPPIES.

LEASH TRAINING

House-training and leash training go hand in hand, literally. When taking your puppy outside to do his business, lead him there on his leash. Unless an emergency potty run is called for, do not whisk the puppy up into your arms and take him outside. If you have a fenced yard, you have the advantage of letting the puppy loose to go out, but it's better to put the dog on the leash and take him to his designated place in the yard until he is reliably house-trained. Taking the puppy for a walk is the best way to house-train a dog. The dog will associate the walk with his time to relieve himself, and the exercise of walking stimulates the dog's bowels and bladder. Dogs that are not trained to relieve themselves on a walk may hold it until they get back home, which of course defeats half the purpose of the walk.

of choice because the floor is washable. Likewise, it's a busy family area that will accustom the pup to a variety of noises, everything from pots and pans to the telephone, blender and dishwasher. He will also be enchanted by the smell of your cooking (and will never be critical when you burn something). An exercise pen (also called an "ex-pen," a puppy version of a playpen) within the room of choice is an excellent means of confinement for a young pup. He can see out and has a certain amount of space in which to run about, but he is safe from dangerous things like electrical cords, heating units, trash baskets or open kitchen-supply cabinets. Place the pen where the puppy will not get a blast of heat or air conditioning.

In the pen, you can put a few toys, his bed (which can be his crate if the dimensions of pen and crate are compatible) and a few layers of newspaper in one small corner, just in case. A water bowl can be hung at a convenient height on the side of the ex-pen so it won't become a splashing pool for an innovative puppy. His food dish can go on the floor, near but not under the water bowl.

Crates are something that pet owners are at last getting used to for their dogs. Wild or domestic canines have always preferred to

SOMEBODY TO BLAME

House-training a puppy can be frustrating for the puppy and the owner alike. The puppy does not instinctively understand the difference between defecating on the pavement outside and on the ceramic tile in the kitchen. He is confused and frightened by his human's exuberant reactions to his natural urges. The owner, arguably the more intelligent of the duo, is also frustrated that he cannot convince his puppy to obey his commands and instructions.

In frustration, the owner may struggle with the temptation to discipline the puppy, scold him or even strike him on the rear end. These harsh corrections are unsuitable and unnecessary, and will defeat your purpose in gaining your puppy's trust and respect. Don't blame your nine-week-old puppy. Blame yourself for not being 100% consistent in the puppy's lessons and routine. The lesson here is simple: try harder and your puppy will succeed.

biscuit for him to chase the first few times. At night, after he's gone outside to potty, he should sleep in his crate. The crate may be kept in his designated area at night or, if you want to be sure to hear those wake-up yips in the morning, put the crate in a corner of your bedroom. However, don't make any response whatsoever to whining or crying. If he's completely ignored, he'll settle down and get to sleep.

Good bedding for a young puppy is an old folded bath towel or an old blanket, something that is easily washable and disposable if necessary ("accidents" will happen!). Never put newspaper in the puppy's crate. Also, those old ideas about adding a clock to replace his mother's heartbeat, or

If a fenced area is not available, you will have to be diligent in taking your dog out on his lead, at the same times each day, for him to relieve himself.

sleep in den-like safe spots, and that is exactly what the crate provides. How often have you seen adult dogs that choose to sleep under a table or chair even though they have full run of the house? It's the den connection.

In your "happy" voice, use the word "Crate" every time you put the pup into his den. If he's new to a crate, toss in a small

a hot-water bottle to replace her warmth, are just that—old ideas. The clock could drive the puppy nuts, and the hot-water bottle could end up as a very soggy waterbed! An extremely good breeder would have introduced your puppy to the crate by letting two pups sleep together for a couple of nights, followed by several nights alone. How thankful you will be if you found that breeder!

Safe toys in the pup's crate or area will keep him occupied, but monitor their condition closely. Discard any toys that show signs of being chewed to bits. Squeaky parts, bits of stuffing or plastic or any other small pieces can cause intestinal blockage or possibly choking if swallowed.

PROGRESSING WITH POTTY-TRAINING
After you've taken your puppy out and he has relieved himself

EXTRA! EXTRA!
The headlines read: "Puppy Piddles Here!" Breeders commonly use newspapers to line their whelping pens, so puppies learn to associate newspapers with relieving themselves. Do not use newspapers to line your pup's crate, as this will signal to your puppy that it is OK to urinate in his crate. If you choose to paper-train your puppy, you will layer newspapers on a section of the floor near the door he uses to go outside. You should encourage the puppy to use the papers to relieve himself, and bring him there whenever you see him getting ready to go. Little by little, you will reduce the size of the newspaper-covered area so that the puppy will learn to relieve himself "on the other side of the door."

A small crate like this is fine for a pup, but he will outgrow it quickly. It is wise to buy a crate from the outset that is large enough for a fully grown Welsh.

in the area you've selected, he can have some free time with the family as long as there is someone responsible for watching him. That doesn't mean just someone in the same room who is watching TV or busy on the computer, but one person who is doing nothing other than keeping an eye on the pup, playing with him on the floor and helping him understand his position in the pack.

This first taste of freedom will let you begin to set the house rules. If you don't want the dog on the furniture, now is the time to prevent his first attempts to jump up onto the couch. The word to use in this case is "Off," not "Down." "Down" is the word you will use to teach the down position, which is something entirely different.

Most corrections at this stage come in the form of simply distracting the puppy. Instead of telling him "No" for "Don't chew the carpet," distract the chomping puppy with a toy and he'll forget about the carpet.

As you are playing with the pup, do not forget to watch him closely and pay attention to his body language. Whenever you see him begin to circle or sniff, take the puppy outside to relieve himself. If you are paper-training, put him back into his confined area on the newspapers. In either case, praise him as he eliminates while he actually is *in the act* of relieving himself. Three seconds after he has finished is too late! You'll be praising him for running toward you, picking up a toy or whatever he may be doing at that moment, and that's not what you want to be praising him for. Timing is a vital tool in all dog training. Use it.

Remove soiled newspapers immediately and replace them with clean ones. You may want to take a small piece of soiled paper and place it in the middle of the new clean papers, as the scent will attract him to that spot

when it's time to go again. That scent attraction is why it's so important to clean up any messes made in the house by using a product specially made to eliminate the odor of dog urine and droppings. Regular household cleansers won't do the trick. Pet shops sell the best pet deodorizers. Invest in the largest container you can find.

Scent attraction eventually will lead your pup to his chosen spot outdoors; this is the basis of outdoor training. When you take your puppy outside to relieve himself, use a one-word command such as "Outside" or "Go-potty"

POTTY COMMAND

Most dogs love to please their masters; there are no bounds to what dogs will do to make their owners happy. The potty command is a good example of this theory. If toileting on command makes the master happy, then more power to him. Puppies will obligingly piddle if it really makes their keepers smile. Some owners can be creative about which word they will use to command their dogs to relieve themselves. Some popular choices are "Potty," "Tinkle," "Piddle," "Let's go," "Hurry up" and "Toilet." Give the command every time your puppy goes into position and the puppy will begin to associate his business with the command.

BE UPSTANDING!

You are the dog's leader. During training, stand up straight so your dog looks up at you, and therefore up *to* you. Say the command words distinctly, in a clear, declarative tone of voice. (No barking!) Give rewards only as the correct response takes place (remember your timing!). Praise, smiles and treats are "rewards" used to positively reinforce correct responses. Don't repeat a mistake. Just change to another exercise—you will soon find success!

(that's one word to the puppy!) as you pick him up and attach his leash. Then put him down in his area. If for any reason you can't carry him, snap the leash on quickly and lead him to his spot. Now comes the hard part—hard for you, that is. Just stand there until he urinates and defecates. Move him a few feet in one direction or another if he's just sitting there looking at you, but remember that this is neither playtime nor time for a walk. This is strictly a business trip! Then, as he circles and squats (remember your timing!), give him a quiet "Good dog" as praise. If you start to jump for joy, ecstatic over his performance, he'll do one of two things: either he will stop midstream, as it were, or he'll do it again for you—in the house—and expect you to be just as delighted!

Give him five minutes or so and, if he doesn't go in that time, take him back indoors to his confined area and try again in another ten minutes, or immediately if you see him sniffing and circling. By careful observation, you'll soon work out a successful schedule.

Accidents, by the way, are just that—accidents. Clean them up quickly and thoroughly, without comment, after the puppy has been taken outside to finish his business and then put back into his area or crate. If you witness an accident in progress, say "No!" in a stern voice and get the pup outdoors immediately. No punishment is needed. You and your puppy are just learning each other's language, and sometimes it's easy to miss a puppy's message. Chalk it up to experience and watch more closely from now on.

KEEPING THE PACK ORDERLY
Discipline is a form of training that brings order to life. For example, military discipline is what allows the soldiers in an army to work as one. Discipline is a form of teaching and, in dogs, is the basis of how the successful pack operates. Each member knows his place in the pack and all respect the leader, or Alpha dog. It is essential for your puppy that you establish this type of relationship, with you as the

Alpha, or leader. It is a form of social coexistence that all canines recognize and accept. Discipline, therefore, is never to be confused with punishment. When you teach your puppy how you want him to behave, and he behaves properly and you praise him for it, you are disciplining him with a form of positive reinforcement.

For a dog, rewards come in the form of praise, a smile, a cheerful tone of voice, a few friendly pats or a rub of the ears. Rewards are also small food treats. Obviously, that does not mean bits of regular dog food. Instead, treats are very small bits of special things like cheese or pieces of soft dog treats. The idea is to reward the dog with something very small that he can taste and swallow, providing instant positive reinforcement. If he has to take time to chew the treat, he will have forgotten what he did to earn it by the time he is finished.

Your puppy should never be physically punished. The displeasure shown on your face and in your voice is sufficient to signal to the pup that he has done something wrong. He wants to please everyone higher up on the social ladder, especially his leader, so a scowl and harsh voice will take care of the error. Growling out the word "Shame!" when the pup is caught in the act

of doing something wrong is better than the repetitive "No." Some dogs hear "No" so often that they begin to think it's their name! By the way, do not use the dog's name when you're correcting him. His name is reserved to get his attention for something pleasant about to take place.

Welsh Terriers are a food-motivated bunch, something that owners can use to their advantage in training.

There are punishments that have nothing to do with you. For example, your dog may think that chasing cats is one reason for his existence. You can try to stop it as much as you like but without success, because it's such fun for the dog. But one good hissing, spitting, swipe of a cat's claws across the dog's nose will put an end to the game forever.

A sturdy leash and collar, a good attitude and a willing Welsh are key ingredients in training success.

Intervene only when your dog's eyeball is seriously at risk. Cat scratches can cause permanent damage to an innocent but annoying puppy.

PUPPY KINDERGARTEN

COLLAR AND LEASH

Before you begin your Welsh Terrier puppy's education, he must be used to his collar and leash. Choose a collar for your puppy that is secure, but not heavy or bulky. He won't enjoy training if he's uncomfortable. A flat buckle collar is fine for every-day wear and for initial puppy training. For older dogs, there are several types of training collars such as the martingale, which is a double loop that tightens slightly around the neck, or the head collar, which is similar to a horse's halter. Do not use a chain choke collar with your Welsh Terrier. It is neither necessary nor effective.

A lightweight 6-foot woven cotton training leash is preferred by most trainers because it is easy to fold up in your hand and comfortable to hold because there is a certain amount of give to it. There are lessons where the dog will start off 6 feet away from you at the end of the leash. The leash used to take the puppy outside to relieve himself is shorter because you don't want him to roam away from his area. The shorter leash will also be the one to use when you walk the puppy.

If you've been wise enough to enroll in a Puppy Kindergarten training class, suggestions will be made as to the best collar and leash for your young puppy. I say "wise" because your puppy will be in a class with puppies in his age range (up to five months old) of all breeds and sizes. It's the perfect way for him to learn the right way (and the wrong way) to interact with other dogs as well as their people. You cannot teach your puppy how to interpret another dog's sign language. For a first-time puppy owner, these socialization classes are invaluable. For experienced dog owners, they are a real boon to further training.

SMILE WHEN YOU ORDER ME AROUND!

While trainers recommend practicing with your dog every day, it's perfectly acceptable to take a "mental health day" off. It's better not to train the dog on days when you're in a sour mood. Your bad attitude or lack of interest will be sensed by your dog, and he will respond accordingly. Studies show that dogs are well tuned in to their humans' emotions. Be conscious of how you use your voice when talking to your dog. Raising your voice or shouting will only erode your dog's trust in you as his trainer and master.

ATTENTION

You've been using the dog's name since the minute you collected him from the breeder, so you should be able to get his attention by saying his name—with a big smile and in an excited tone of voice. His response will be the puppy equivalent of "Here I am! What are we going to do?" Your immediate response (if you haven't guessed by now) is "Good dog." Rewarding him at the moment he pays attention to you teaches him the proper way to respond when he hears his name.

EXERCISES FOR A BASIC CANINE EDUCATION

THE SIT EXERCISE

There are several ways to teach the puppy to sit. The first one is to catch him whenever he is about to sit and, as his backside nears the floor, say "Sit, good dog!" That's positive reinforcement and, if your timing is sharp, he will learn that what he's doing at that second is connected to your saying "Sit" and that you think he's clever for doing it!

Another method is to start with the puppy on his leash in front of you. Show him a treat in the palm of your right hand. Bring your hand up under his nose and, almost in slow motion, move your hand up and back so his nose goes up in the air and

Once your pup is comfortable with his collar and lead and you're ready to start with basic commands, the sit exercise is the first you will teach.

his head tilts back as he follows the treat in your hand. At that point, he will have to either sit or fall over, so as his back legs buckle under, say "Sit, good dog," and then give him the treat and lots of praise. You may have to begin with your hand lightly running up his chest, actually lifting his chin up until he sits. Some (usually older) dogs require gentle pressure on their hindquarters with the left hand, in which case the dog should be on your left side. Puppies generally do not appreciate this physical dominance.

After a few times, you should be able to show the dog a treat in the open palm of your hand, raise your hand waist-high as you say "Sit" and have him sit. You will thereby have taught him two things at the same time. Both the verbal command and the motion of the hand are signals for the sit. Your puppy is watching you almost more than he is listening to you, so what you do is just as important as what you say.

Don't save any of these drills only for training sessions. Use them as much as possible at odd times during a normal day. The dog should always sit before being given his food dish. He should sit to let you go through a doorway first, when the doorbell rings or when you stop to speak to someone on the street.

THE DOWN EXERCISE

Before beginning to teach the down command, you must consider how the dog feels about this exercise. To him, "down" is a submissive position. Being flat on the floor with you standing over him is not his idea of fun. It's up to you to let him know that, while it may not be fun, the reward of your approval is worth his effort.

Start with the puppy on your left side in a sit position. Hold the leash right above his collar in your left hand. Have an extra-special treat, such as a small piece of cooked chicken or hot dog, in your right hand. Place it at the end of the pup's nose and steadily move your hand down and forward along the ground.

A SIMPLE "SIT"

When you command your dog to sit, use the word "Sit." Do not say "Sit down," as your dog will not know whether you mean "Sit" or "Down," or maybe you mean both. Be clear in your instructions to your dog; use one-word commands and always be consistent.

Hold the leash to prevent a sudden lunge for the food. As the puppy goes into the down position, say "Down" very gently.

The difficulty with this exercise is twofold: it's both the submissive aspect and the fact that most people say the word "Down" as if they were a drill sergeant in charge of recruits! So issue the command sweetly, give him the treat and have the pup maintain the down position for several seconds. If he tries to get up immediately, place your hands on his shoulders and press down gently, giving him a very quiet "Good dog." As you progress with this lesson, increase the "down time" until he will hold it until you say "Okay" (his cue for release). Practice this one in the house at various times throughout the day.

By increasing the length of time during which the dog must maintain the down position, you'll find many uses for it. For example, he can lie at your feet in the vet's office or anywhere that both of you have to wait, when you are on the phone, while the family is eating and so forth. If you progress to training for competitive obedience, he'll already be all set for the exercise called the "long down."

THE STAY EXERCISE

You can teach your Welsh Terrier to stay in the sit, down and stand

Before progressing to the down/stay, the dog must be comfortable with the down command.

that you walk away from him before turning until you reach the length of your training leash. But don't rush it! Go back to the beginning if he moves before he should. No matter what lesson you are teaching, never be upset by having to back up for a few days. The repetition and practice are what will make your dog reliable in these commands. It won't do any good to move on to something more difficult if the command is not mastered at the easier levels. Above all, even if you do get frustrated, never let

positions. To teach the sit/stay, have the dog sit on your left side. Hold the leash at waist level in your left hand and let the dog know that you have a treat in your closed right hand. Step forward on your right foot as you say "Stay." Immediately turn and stand directly in front of the dog, keeping your right hand up high so he'll keep his eye on the treat hand and maintain the sit position for a count of five. Return to your original position and offer the reward.

Increase the length of the sit/stay each time until the dog can hold it for at least 30 seconds without moving. After about a week of success, move out on your right foot and take two steps before turning to face the dog. Give the "Stay" hand signal (left palm back toward the dog's head) as you leave. He gets the treat when you return and he holds the sit/stay. Increase the distance

TIPS FOR TRAINING AND SAFETY

1. Whether on- or off-leash, practice only in a fenced area.
2. Remove the training collar when the training session is over.
3. Don't try to break up a dogfight.
4. "Come," "Leave it" and "Wait" are safety commands.
5. The dog belongs in a crate or behind a barrier when riding in the car.
6. Don't ignore the dog's first sign of aggression. Aggression only gets worse, so take it seriously.
7. Keep the faces of children and dogs separated.
8. Pay attention to what the dog is chewing.
9. Keep the vet's number near your phone.
10. "Okay" is a useful release command.

your puppy know! Always keep a positive, upbeat attitude during training, which will transmit to your dog for positive results.

The down/stay is taught in the same way once the dog is completely reliable and steady with the down command. Again, don't rush it. With the dog in the down position on your left side, step out on your right foot as you say "Stay." Return by walking around in back of the dog and into your original position. While you are training, it's okay to murmur something like "Hold on" to encourage him to stay put. When the dog will stay without moving when you are at a distance of 3 or 4 feet, begin to increase the length of time before you return. Be sure he holds the down on your return until you say "Okay." At that point, he gets his treat—just so he'll remember for next time that it's not over until it's over.

THE COME EXERCISE

No command is more important to the safety of your Welsh Terrier than "Come." It is what you should say every single time you see the puppy running toward you: "Binky, come! Good dog." During playtime, run a few feet away from the puppy and then turn and tell him to "Come" as he is already running to you. You can go so far as to teach your puppy two things at once if you squat

> ### OKAY!
> This is the signal that tells your dog that he can quit whatever he was doing. Use "Okay" to end a session on a correct response to a command. (Never end on an incorrect response.) Lots of praise follows. People use "Okay" a lot and it has other uses for dogs, too. Your dog is barking. You say, "Okay! Come!" "Okay" signals him to stop the barking activity and "Come" allows him to come to you for a "Good dog."

down and hold out your arms. As the pup gets close to you and you're saying "Good dog," bring your right arm in about waist high. Now he's also learning the hand signal, an excellent device should you be on the phone when you need to get him to come to you! You'll also both be one step

The trainer uses both verbal commands and hand signals in teaching the stay. Distance and time are increased gradually as the dog learns.

LET'S GO!

Many people use "Let's go" instead of "Heel" when teaching their dogs to behave on lead. It sounds more like fun! When beginning to teach the heel, whatever command you use, always step off on your left foot. That's the one next to the dog, who is on your left side, in case you've forgotten. Keep a loose leash. When the dog pulls ahead, stop, bring him back and begin again. Use treats to guide him around turns.

ahead when you enter obedience classes.

When the puppy responds to your well-timed "Come," try it with the puppy on the training leash. This time, catch him off guard, while he's sniffing a leaf or watching a bird: "Binky, come!" You may have to pause for a split second after his name to be sure you have his attention. If the puppy shows any sign of confusion, give the leash a mild jerk and take a couple of steps backward. Do not repeat the command. In this case, you should say "Good come" as he reaches you.

That's the number-one rule of training. Each command word is given just once. Anything more is nagging. You'll also notice that all commands are one word only. Even when they are actually two words, you say them as one.

Never call the dog to come to you—with or without his name—if you are angry or intend to correct him for some misbehavior. When correcting the pup, you go to him. Your dog must always connect "Come" with something pleasant and with your approval; then you can rely on his response. Always greet his coming to you with plenty of happy praise.

Puppies, like children, have notoriously short attention spans, so don't overdo it with any of the training. Keep each lesson short.

Break it up with a quick run around the yard or a ball toss, repeat the lesson and quit as soon as the pup gets it right. That way, you will always end with a "Good dog."

Life isn't perfect and neither are puppies. A time will come, often around ten months of age, when he'll become "selectively deaf" or choose to "forget" his name. He may respond by wagging his tail (and even seeming to smile at you) with a look that says "Make me!" Laugh, throw his favorite toy and skip the lesson you had planned. Pups will be pups!

THE HEEL EXERCISE

The second most important command to teach, after the come, is the heel. When you are walking your growing puppy, you need to be in control. Besides, it looks terrible to be pulled and yanked down the street, and it's not much fun either. Your nine- to ten-week-old puppy will probably follow you everywhere, but that's his natural instinct, not your control over the situation. However, any time he does follow you, you can say "Heel" and be ahead of the game, as he will learn to associate this command with the action of following you before you even begin teaching him to heel.

There is a very precise, almost military, procedure for teaching your dog to heel. As with all other obedience training, begin with the dog on your left side. He will be in a very nice sit and you will have the training leash across your chest. Hold the loop and folded leash in your right hand. Pick up the slack leash above the dog in your left hand and hold it loosely at your side. Step out on your left foot as you say "Heel." If the puppy does not move, give a gentle tug or pat your left leg to get him started. If he surges ahead of you, stop and pull him back gently until he is at your side. Tell him to sit and begin again.

Walk a few steps and stop while the puppy is correctly beside you. Tell him to sit and give mild verbal praise. (More enthusiastic praise will encourage him to think the lesson is over.)

A tasty tidbit for a job well done! Verbal praise is even more important, so don't forget to also tell your Welsh what a good dog he is.

time and free-running exercise to shake off the stress when the lessons are over. You don't want him to associate training with all work and no fun.

OBEDIENCE CLASSES
The advantages of an obedience class are that your dog will have to learn amid the distractions of other people and dogs and that your mistakes will be quickly corrected by the trainer. Teaching your dog along with a qualified instructor and other handlers who may have more dog experience than you is another plus of the class environment. The instructor and other handlers can help you to find the most efficient way of teaching your dog a command or

The first Welsh to be awarded the Master Agility Champion (MACH) is Webster, MACH Cisseldale's Double Trouble CGC, owned by Linda and Brad Brisbin and bred by Barbara Cissel. Webster was the top Agility Welsh for 2001–2004.

Repeat the lesson, increasing the number of steps you take only as long as the dog is heeling nicely beside you. When you end the lesson, have him hold the sit and then give him the "Okay" to let him know that this is the end of the lesson. Praise him so that he knows he did a good job.

The cure for excessive pulling (a common problem) is to stop when the dog is no more than 2 or 3 feet ahead of you. Guide him back into position and begin again. With a really determined puller, try switching to a head collar. This will automatically turn the pup's head toward you so you can bring him back easily to the heel position. Give quiet, reassuring praise every time the leash goes slack and he's staying with you.

Staying and heeling can take a lot out of a dog, so provide play-

NO MORE TREATS!
When your dog is responding promptly and correctly to commands, it's time to eliminate treats. Begin by alternating a treat reward with a verbal-praise-only reward. Gradually eliminate all treats while increasing the frequency of praise. Overlook pleading eyes and expectant expressions, but if he's still watching your treat hand, you're on your way to using hand signals.

exercise. It's often easier to learn from other people's mistakes than your own. You will also learn all of the requirements for competitive obedience trials, in which you can earn titles and go on to advanced jumping and retrieving exercises, which are fun for many dogs. Obedience classes build the foundation needed for many other canine activities (in which we humans are allowed to participate, too!).

TRAINING FOR OTHER ACTIVITIES

Once your dog has basic obedience under his collar and is 12 months of age, you can enter the world of agility training. Dogs think agility is pure fun, like being turned loose in an amusement park full of obstacles! In addition to agility, your Welsh may enjoy participating in go-to-ground events for terriers and/or tracking, which is open to all "nosey" dogs (which would include all dogs!). For those who like to volunteer, there is the wonderful feeling of owning a therapy dog and visiting hospices, nursing homes and veterans' homes to bring smiles, comfort and companionship to those who live there.

Around the house, your Welsh Terrier can be taught to do some simple chores. You might teach him to carry a small basket or to fetch the morning newspaper. The kids can teach the dog all kinds of tricks, from playing hide-and-seek to balancing a biscuit on his nose. The Welsh will enjoy joining you on outings and hikes; a long lead will let him explore safely and keep him from going off "on the hunt." A family dog is what rounds out the family. Everything he does, including sitting in your lap or gazing lovingly at you, represents the bonus of owning a dog.

We thought that the Welsh Terrier was an earthdog, not a water dog! Every Welsh has individual likes and aptitudes, so find out what your dog enjoys and have a great time together.

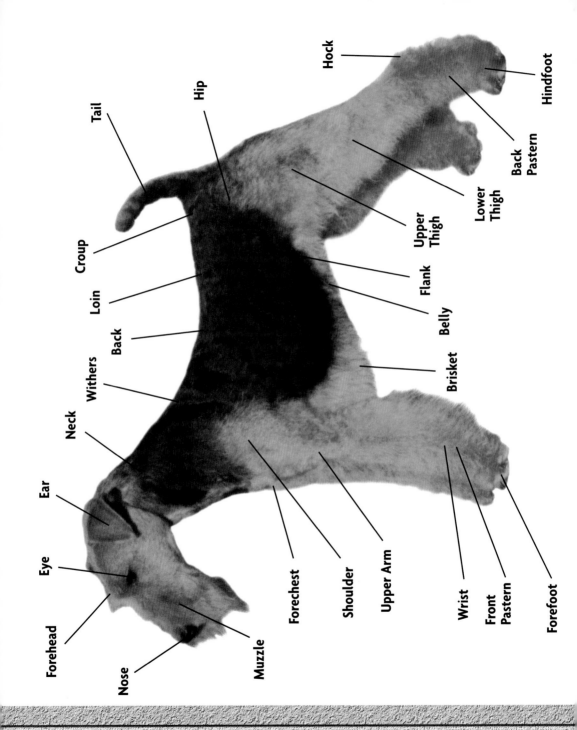

Hock

Hindfoot

Hip

Tail

Back Pastern

Lower Thigh

Upper Thigh

Croup

Flank

Loin

Belly

Back

Withers

Brisket

Neck

Ear

Eye

Forehead

Nose

Muzzle

Forechest

Shoulder

Upper Arm

Wrist

Front Pastern

Forefoot

PHYSICAL STRUCTURE OF THE WELSH TERRIER

HEALTHCARE OF YOUR

WELSH TERRIER

By Lowell Ackerman DVM, DACVD

HEALTHCARE FOR A LIFETIME

When you own a dog, you become his healthcare advocate over his entire lifespan, as well as being the one to shoulder the financial burden of such care. Accordingly, it is worthwhile to focus on prevention rather than treatment, as you and your pet will both be happier.

Of course, the best place to have begun your program of preventive healthcare is with the initial purchase or adoption of your dog. There is no way of guaranteeing that your new furry friend is free of medical problems, but there are some things you can do to improve your odds. You certainly should have done adequate research into the Welsh Terrier and have selected your puppy carefully rather than buying on impulse. Health issues aside, a large number of pet abandonment and relinquishment cases arise from a mismatch between pet needs and owner expectations. This is entirely preventable with appropriate planning and finding a good breeder.

Regarding healthcare issues specifically, it is very difficult to make blanket statements about where to acquire a problem-free pet, but, again, a reputable breeder is your best bet. In an ideal situation, you have the opportunity to see both parents, get references from other owners of the breeder's pups and see genetic-testing documentation for several generations of the litter's ancestors. At the very least, you must thoroughly investigate the Welsh Terrier and the problems inherent in the breed, as well as the genetic testing available to screen for those problems. Genetic testing offers some important benefits, but testing is available for only a few disorders in a relatively small number of breeds and is not available for some of the most common genetic diseases, such as hip dysplasia, cataracts, epilepsy, cardiomyopathy, etc. This area of research is indeed exciting and increasingly important, and advances will continue to be made each year. In fact, recent research has shown that there is an equivalent dog gene for

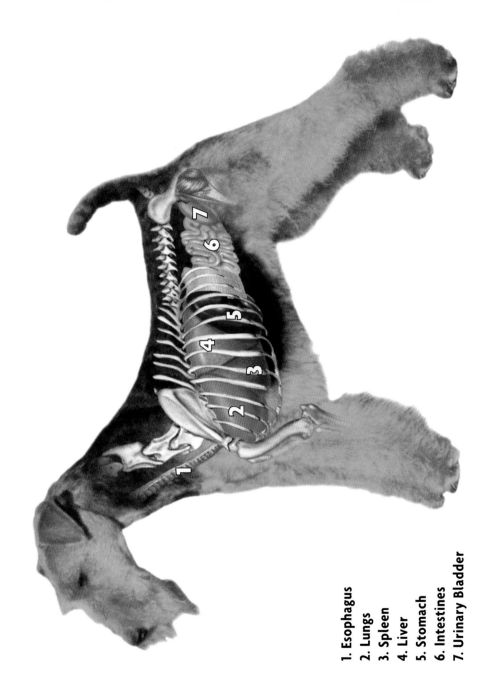

1. Esophagus
2. Lungs
3. Spleen
4. Liver
5. Stomach
6. Intestines
7. Urinary Bladder

INTERNAL ORGANS OF THE WELSH TERRIER

75% of known human genes, so research done in either species is likely to benefit the other.

We've also discussed that evaluating the behavioral nature of your Welsh Terrier and that of his immediate family members is an important part of the selection process that cannot be underestimated or overemphasized. It is sometimes difficult to evaluate temperament in puppies because certain behavioral tendencies, such as some forms of aggression, may not be immediately evident. More dogs are euthanized each year for behavioral reasons than for all medical conditions combined, so it is critical to take temperament issues seriously. Start with a well-balanced, friendly companion and put the time and effort into proper socialization, and you will both be rewarded with a lifelong valued relationship.

Assuming that you have started off with a pup from healthy, sound stock, you then become responsible for helping your veterinarian keep your pet healthy. Some crucial things happen before you even bring your puppy home. Parasite control typically begins at two weeks of age, and vaccinations typically begin at six to eight weeks of age. A pre-pubertal evaluation is typically scheduled for about six months of age. At this time, a dental evaluation is done

> **DOGGIE DENTAL DON'TS**
> A veterinary dental exam is necessary if you notice one or any combination of the following in your dog:
> • Broken, loose or missing teeth
> • Loss of appetite (which could be due to mouth pain or illness caused by infection)
> • Gum abnormalities, including redness, swelling and bleeding
> • Drooling, with or without blood
> • Yellowing of the teeth or gumline, indicating tartar
> • Bad breath

(since the adult teeth are now in), heartworm prevention is started and neutering or spaying is most commonly done.

It is critical to commence regular dental care at home if you have not already done so. It may not sound very important, but most dogs have active periodontal disease by four years of age if they don't have their teeth cleaned regularly at home, not just at their veterinary exams. Dental problems lead to more than just bad "doggie breath." Gum disease can have very serious medical consequences. If you start brushing your dog's teeth and using antiseptic rinses from a young age, your dog will be accustomed to it and will not resist. The results will be healthy dentition, which your pet will need to enjoy a long, healthy life.

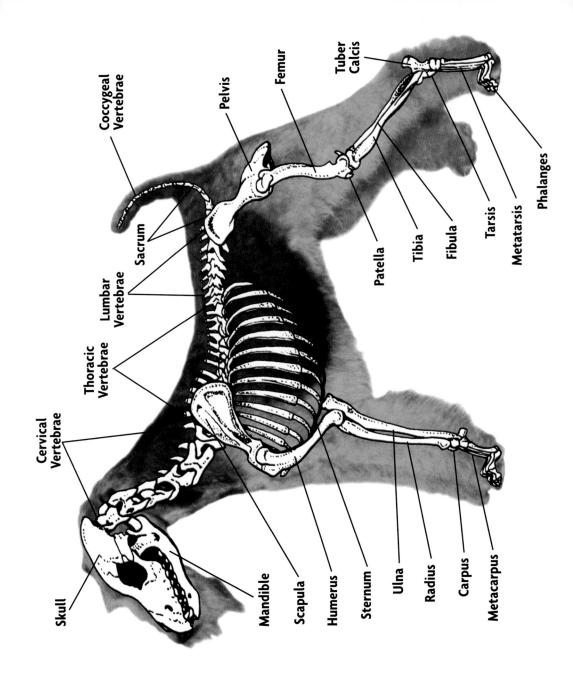

Coccygeal
Vertebrae

Pelvis

Femur

Tuber
Calcis

Phalanges

Metatarsis

Tarsis

Fibula

Tibia

Patella

Sacrum

Lumbar
Vertebrae

Thoracic
Vertebrae

Cervical
Vertebrae

Skull

Mandible

Scapula

Humerus

Sternum

Ulna

Radius

Carpus

Metacarpus

Skeletal Structure of the Welsh Terrier

Most dogs are considered adults at a year of age, although the Welsh Terrier continues to mature up to about the age of two. Even individual dogs within each breed have different healthcare requirements, so work with your veterinarian to determine what will be needed and what your role should be. This doctor-client relationship is important, because as vaccination guidelines change, there may not be an annual "vaccine visit" scheduled. You must make sure that you see your veterinarian at least annually, even if no vaccines are due, because this is the best opportunity to coordinate healthcare activities and to make sure that no medical issues creep by unaddressed.

When your Welsh Terrier reaches three-quarters of his anticipated lifespan, he is considered a "senior" and likely requires some special care. In general, if you've been taking great care of your canine companion throughout his formative and adult years, the transition to senior status should be a smooth one. Age is not a disease, and as long as everything is functioning as it should, there is no reason why most of late adulthood should not be rewarding for both you and your pet. This is especially true if you have tended to the details, such as regular veterinary visits, proper dental care, excellent nutrition

and management of bone and joint issues.

At this stage in your Welsh Terrier's life, your veterinarian may want to schedule visits twice yearly, instead of once, to run some laboratory screenings, electrocardiograms and the like, and to change the diet to something more digestible. Catching problems early is the best way to manage them effectively. Treating

TAKING YOUR DOG'S TEMPERATURE

It is important to know how to take your dog's temperature at times when you think he may be ill. It's not the most enjoyable task, but it can be done without too much difficulty. It's easier with a helper, preferably someone with whom the dog is friendly, so that one of you can hold the dog while the other inserts the thermometer.

Before inserting the thermometer, coat the end with petroleum jelly. Insert the thermometer slowly and gently into the dog's rectum about one inch. Wait for the reading—digital thermometers will register in less than a minute. Be sure to remove the thermometer carefully and clean it thoroughly after each use.

A dog's normal body temperature is between 100.5 and 102.5 degrees F. Immediate veterinary attention is required if the dog's temperature is below 99 or above 104 degrees F.

YOUR DOG NEEDS TO VISIT THE VET IF:

- He has ingested a toxin such as antifreeze or a toxic plant; in these cases, administer first aid and call the vet right away
- His teeth are discolored, loose or missing or he has sores or other signs of infection or abnormality in the mouth
- He has been vomiting, has had diarrhea or has been constipated for over 24 hours; call immediately if you notice blood
- He has refused food for over 24 hours
- His eating habits, water intake or toilet habits have noticeably changed; if you have noticed weight gain or weight loss
- He shows symptoms of bloat, which requires immediate attention
- He is salivating excessively
- He has a lump in his throat
- He has a lump or bumps anywhere on the body
- He is very lethargic
- He appears to be in pain or otherwise has trouble chewing or swallowing
- His skin loses elasticity

Of course there will be other instances in which a visit to the vet is necessary; these are just some of the signs that could be indicative of serious problems that need to be caught as early as possible.

the early stages of heart disease is so much easier than trying to intervene when there is more significant damage to the heart muscle. Similarly, managing the beginning of kidney problems is fairly routine if there is no significant kidney damage. Other problems, like cognitive dysfunction (similar to senility and Alzheimer's disease), cancer, diabetes and arthritis, are more common in older dogs, but all can be treated to help the dog live as many happy, comfortable years as possible. Just as in people, medical management is more effective (and less expensive) when you catch things early.

SELECTING A VETERINARIAN

There is probably no more important decision that you will make regarding your pet's healthcare than the selection of his doctor. Your pet's veterinarian will be a pediatrician, family-practice physician and gerontologist, depending on the dog's life stage, and will be the individual who makes recommendations regarding issues such as when specialists need to be consulted, when diagnostic testing and/or therapeutic intervention is needed and when you will need to seek outside emergency and critical-care services. Your vet will act as your advocate and liaison throughout these processes.

Everyone has his own idea about what to look for in a vet, an individual who will play a big role in his dog's (and, of course, his own) life for many years to come. For some, it is the compassionate caregiver with whom they hope to develop a professional relationship to span the lifetime of their dogs and even their future pets. For others, they are seeking a clinician with keen diagnostic and therapeutic insight who can deliver state-of-the-art healthcare. Still others need a veterinary facility that is open evenings and weekends, is in close proximity or provides mobile veterinary services to accommodate their schedules; these people may not much mind that their dogs might see different veterinarians on each visit. Just as we have different reasons for selecting our own healthcare professionals (e.g., covered by insurance plan, expert in field, convenient location, etc.), we should not expect that there is a one-size-fits-all recommendation for selecting a veterinarian and veterinary practice. The best advice is to be honest in your assessment of what you expect from a veterinary practice and to conscientiously research the options in your area. You will quickly appreciate that not all veterinary practices are the same, and you will be happiest with one that truly meets your needs.

There is another point to be considered in the selection of veterinary services. Not that long ago, a single veterinarian would attempt to manage all medical and surgical issues as they arose. That was often problematic, because veterinarians are trained in many species and many

AIRBORNE ALLERGIES

Just as humans have hay fever, rose fever and other fevers from which they suffer during the pollinating season, many dogs suffer from the same allergies, and these commonly plague some Welsh Terriers. When the pollen count is high, your dog might suffer, but don't expect him to sneeze and have a runny nose like a human would. Dogs react to pollen allergies the same way they react to fleas— they scratch and bite themselves. Dogs, like humans, can be tested for allergens. Discuss the testing with your veterinary dermatologist.

diseases, and it was just impossible for general veterinary practitioners to be experts in every species, every breed, every field and every ailment. However, just as in the human healthcare fields, specialization has allowed general practitioners to concentrate on primary healthcare delivery, especially wellness and the prevention of infectious diseases, and to utilize a network of specialists to assist in the management of conditions that require specific expertise and experience. Thus there are now many types of veterinary specialists, including dermatologists, cardiologists, ophthalmologists, surgeons, internists, oncologists, neurologists, behaviorists, criticalists and others to help primary-care veterinarians deal with complicated medical challenges. In most cases, specialists see cases referred by primary-care veterinarians, make diagnoses and set up management plans. From there, the animals' ongoing care is returned to their primary-care veterinarians. This important team approach to your pet's medical-care needs has provided opportunities for advanced care and an unparalleled level of quality to be delivered.

With all of the opportunities for your Welsh Terrier to receive high-quality veterinary medical care, there is another topic that needs to be addressed at the same time—cost. It's been said that you can have excellent healthcare or inexpensive healthcare, but never both; this is as true in veterinary medicine as it is in human medicine. While veterinary costs are a fraction of what the same services cost in

PROBLEM: AND THAT STARTS WITH "P"

Urinary tract problems more commonly affect female dogs, especially those who have been spayed. The first sign that a urinary tract problem exists usually is a strong odor from the urine or an unusual color. Blood in the urine, known as hematuria, is another sign of an infection, related to cystitis, a bladder infection, bladder cancer or a blood-clotting disorder. Urinary tract problems can also be signaled by the dog's straining while urinating, experiencing pain during urination and genital discharge as well as excessive water intake and urination.

Excessive drinking, in and of itself, does not indicate a urinary tract problem. A dog who is drinking more than normal may have a kidney or liver problem, a hormonal disorder or diabetes mellitus. Behaviorists report a disorder known as psychogenic polydipsia, which manifests itself in excessive drinking and urination. If you notice your dog drinking much more than normal, take him to the vet.

the human healthcare arena, it is still difficult to deal with unanticipated medical costs, especially since they can easily creep into hundreds or even thousands of dollars if specialists or emergency services become involved. However, there are ways of managing these risks. The easiest is to buy pet health insurance and realize that its foremost purpose is not to cover routine healthcare visits but rather to serve as an umbrella for those rainy days when your pet needs medical care and you don't want to worry about whether or not you can afford that care.

Pet insurance policies are very cost-effective (and very inexpensive by human health-insurance standards), but make sure that you buy the policy long before you intend to use it (preferably starting in puppyhood, because coverage will exclude pre-existing conditions) and that you are actually buying an indemnity insurance plan from an insurance company that is regulated by your state or province. Many insurance policy look-alikes are actually discount clubs that are redeemable only at specific locations and for specific services. An indemnity plan covers your pet at almost all veterinary, specialty and emergency practices and is an excellent way to manage your pet's ongoing healthcare needs.

VACCINATIONS AND INFECTIOUS DISEASES

There has never been an easier time to prevent a variety of infectious diseases in your dog, but the advances we've made in veterinary medicine come with a price—choice. Now while it may seem that choice is a good thing (and it is), it has never been more difficult for the pet owner (or the veterinarian) to make an informed decision about the best way to protect pets through vaccination.

Years ago, it was just accepted that puppies got a starter series of vaccinations and then annual "boosters" throughout their lives to keep them protected. As more and more vaccines became available, consumers wanted the convenience of having all of that protection in a single injection. The result was "multivalent" vaccines that crammed a lot of protection into a single syringe. The manufacturers' recommendations were to give the vaccines annually, and this was a simple enough protocol to follow. However, as veterinary medicine has become more sophisticated and we have started looking more at healthcare quandaries rather than convenience, it became necessary to reevaluate the situation and deal with some tough questions. It is important to realize that whether or not to use a particular vaccine depends on the risk of contracting the disease against which it protects, the severity of

COMMON INFECTIOUS DISEASES

Let's discuss some of the diseases that create the need for vaccination in the first place. Following are the major canine infectious diseases and a simple explanation of each.

Rabies: A devastating viral disease that can be fatal in dogs and people. In fact, vaccination of dogs and cats is an important public-health measure to create a resistant animal buffer population to protect people from contracting the disease. Vaccination schedules are determined on a government level and are not optional for pet owners; rabies vaccination is required by law in all 50 states.

Parvovirus: A severe, potentially life-threatening disease that is easily transmitted between dogs. There are four strains of the virus, but it is believed that there is significant "cross-protection" between strains that may be included in individual vaccines.

Distemper: A potentially severe and life-threatening disease with a relatively high risk of exposure, especially in certain regions. In very high-risk distemper environments, young pups may be vaccinated with human measles vaccine, a related virus that offers cross-protection when administered at four to ten weeks of age.

Hepatitis: Caused by canine adenovirus type 1 (CAV-1), but since vaccination with the causative virus has a higher rate of adverse effects, cross-protection is derived from the use of adenovirus type 2 (CAV-2), a cause of respiratory disease and one of the potential causes of canine cough. Vaccination with CAV-2 provides long-term immunity against hepatitis, but relatively less protection against respiratory infection.

Canine cough: Also called tracheobronchitis, actually a fairly complicated result of viral and bacterial offenders; therefore, even with vaccination, protection is incomplete. Wherever dogs congregate, canine cough will likely be spread among them. Intranasal vaccination with *Bordetella* and parainfluenza is the best safeguard, but the duration of immunity does not appear to be very long, typically a year at most. These are non-core vaccines, but vaccination is sometimes mandated by boarding kennels, obedience classes, dog shows and other places where dogs congregate to try to minimize spread of infection.

Leptospirosis: A potentially fatal disease that is more common in some geographic regions. It is capable of being spread to humans. The disease varies with the individual "serovar," or strain, of *Leptospira* involved. Since there does not appear to be much cross-protection between serovars, protection is only as good as the likelihood that the serovar in the vaccine is the same as the one in the pet's local environment. Problems with *Leptospira* vaccines are that protection does not last very long, side effects are not uncommon and a large percentage of dogs (perhaps 30%) may not respond to vaccination.

Borrelia burgdorferi: The cause of Lyme disease, the risk of which varies with the geographic area in which the pet lives and travels. Lyme disease is spread by deer ticks in the eastern US and western black-legged ticks in the western part of the country, and the risk of exposure is high in some regions. Lameness, fever and inappetence are most commonly seen in affected dogs. The extent of protection from the vaccine has not been conclusively demonstrated.

Coronavirus: This disease has a high risk of exposure, especially in areas where dogs congregate, but it typically causes only mild to moderate digestive upset (diarrhea, vomiting, etc.). Vaccines are available, but the duration of protection is believed to be relatively short and the effectiveness of the vaccine in preventing infection is considered low.

There are many other vaccinations available, including those for *Giardia* and canine adenovirus-1. While there may be some specific indications for their use, and local risk factors to be considered, they are not widely recommended for most dogs.

the disease if it is contracted, the duration of immunity provided by the vaccine, the safety of the product and the needs of the individual animal. In a very general sense, rabies, distemper, hepatitis and parvovirus are considered core vaccine needs, while parainfluenza, *Bordetella bronchiseptica*, leptospirosis, coronavirus and borreliosis (Lyme disease) are considered non-core needs and best reserved for animals that demonstrate reasonable risk of contracting the diseases.

NEUTERING/SPAYING

Sterilization procedures (neutering for males/spaying for females) are meant to accomplish several purposes. While the underlying premise is to address the risk of pet overpopulation, there are also some medical and behavioral benefits to the surgeries as well. For females, spaying prior to the first estrus (heat cycle) leads to a marked reduction in the risk of mammary cancer. There also will be no manifestations of "heat" to attract male dogs and no bleeding in the house. For males, there is prevention of testicular cancer and a reduction in the risk of prostate problems. In both sexes, there may be some limited reduction in aggressive behaviors toward other dogs, and some diminishing of urine marking, roaming and mounting.

SAMPLE VACCINATION SCHEDULE

6–8 weeks of age	Parvovirus, Distemper, Adenovirus-2 (Hepatitis)
9–11 weeks of age	Parvovirus, Distemper, Adenovirus-2 (Hepatitis)
12–14 weeks of age	Parvovirus, Distemper, Adenovirus-2 (Hepatitis)
16–20 weeks of age	Rabies
1 year of age	Parvovirus, Distemper, Adenovirus-2 (Hepatitis), Rabies

Revaccination is performed every one to three years, depending on the product, the method of administration and the patient's risk. Initial adult inoculation (for dogs at least 16 weeks of age in which a puppy series was not done or could not be confirmed) is two vaccinations, done three to four weeks apart, with revaccination according to the same criteria mentioned. Other vaccines are given as decided between owner and veterinarian.

While neutering and spaying do indeed prevent animals from contributing to pet overpopulation, even no-cost and low-cost neutering options have not elimi-

nated the problem. Perhaps one of the main reasons for this is that individuals that intentionally breed their dogs and those that allow their animals to run at large are the main causes of unwanted offspring. Also, animals in shelters are often there because they were abandoned or relinquished, not because they came from unplanned matings. Neutering/spaying is important, but it should be considered in the context of the real causes of animals' ending up in shelters and eventually being euthanized.

One of the important considerations regarding neutering is that it is a surgical procedure. This sometimes gets lost in discussions of low-cost procedures and commoditization of the process. In females, spaying is specifically referred to as an ovariohysterectomy. In this procedure, a midline incision is made in the abdomen and the entire uterus and both ovaries are surgically removed. While this is a major invasive surgical procedure, it usually has few complications, because it is typically performed on healthy young animals. However, it is major surgery, as any woman who has had a hysterectomy will attest.

In males, neutering has traditionally referred to castration, which involves the surgical removal of both testicles. While still a significant piece of surgery,

HIT ME WITH A HOT SPOT

What is a hot spot? Technically known as pyotraumatic dermatitis, a hot spot is an infection on the dog's coat, usually by the rear end, under the tail or on a leg, which the dog inflicts upon himself. The dog licks and bites the itchy spot until it becomes inflamed and infected. The hot spot can range in size from the circumference of a grape to the circumference of an apple. Provided that the hot spot is not related to a deeper bacterial infection, it can be treated topically by clipping the area, cleaning the sore and giving prednisone. For bacterial infections, antibiotics are required. In some cases, an Elizabethan collar is required to keep the dog from further irritating the hot spot. The itching can intensify and the pain becomes worse. Medicated shampoos and cool compresses, drying agents and topical steroids may be prescribed by your vet as well.

Hot spots can be caused by fleas, an allergy, an ear infection, anal sac problems, mange or a foreign irritant. Likewise, they can be linked to psychoses. The underlying problem must be addressed in addition to the hot spot itself.

there is not the abdominal exposure that is required in the female surgery. In addition, there is now a chemical sterilization option, in which a solution is injected into each testicle, leading to atrophy of the sperm-producing cells. This can typically be done under sedation rather than full anesthesia. This is a relatively new approach, and there are no long-term clinical studies yet available.

Neutering/spaying is typically done around six months of age at most veterinary hospitals, although techniques have been pioneered to perform the procedures in animals as young as eight weeks of age. In general, the surgeries on the very young animals are done for the specific reason of sterilizing them before they go to their new homes. This is done in some shelter hospitals for assurance that the animals will definitely not produce any pups. Otherwise, these organizations need to rely on owners to comply with their wishes to have the animals "altered" at a later date, something that does not always happen.

There are some exciting immunocontraceptive "vaccines" currently under development, and there may be a time when contraception in pets will not require surgical procedures. We anxiously await these developments.

FOOD ALLERGY

Severe itching, leading to bald patches and open sores on the feet, face, ears, armpits and groin, could be caused by a food allergy. Studies indicate that up to 10% of dogs suffer from food allergies, which develop slowly over time without a change in diet. Dogs who suffer from chronic ear problems may actually have a food allergy. Unfortunately, there are no tests available to determine whether your dog definitely suffers from a food allergy. The dog will be miserable and you will be frustrated and stressed.

Take the problem into your own hands and kitchen. Select a type of meat that your dog is not getting from his existing diet, perhaps white fish, lamb or venison, and prepare a home-cooked food. The food should consist of two parts carbohydrate (rice, pasta or potatoes) and one part protein (the chosen meat). It's better not to start with soy as the protein source unless all of the meats cause a reaction.

Monitor your dog's intake carefully. He must eat only your prepared meal without any treats or side-trips to the garbage can. All family members (and visiting friends) must be informed of the plan. After four or five weeks on the new diet, you will reintroduce a portion of his original diet to determine whether this food is the cause of the skin irritation (or other reactions). Once the dog reacts to the change in diet, resume the new diet. Make dietary modifications every two weeks and keep careful records of any reactions the dog has to the diet.

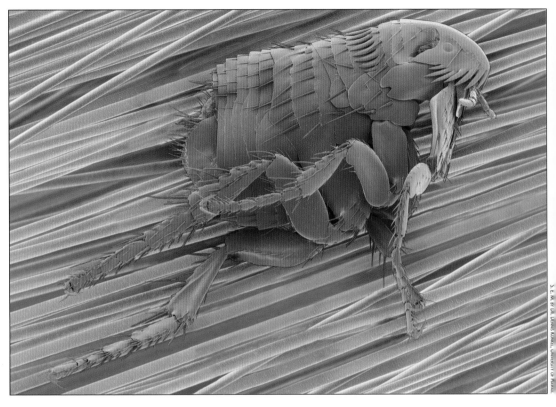

S. E. M. BY DR. DENNIS KUNKEL, UNIVERSITY OF HAWAII

A scanning electron micrograph of a dog flea, Ctenocephalides canis, on dog hair.

EXTERNAL PARASITES

FLEAS

Fleas have been around for millions of years and, while we have better tools now for controlling them than at any time in the past, there still is little chance that they will end up on an endangered species list. Actually, they are very well adapted to living on our pets, and they continue to adapt as we make advances.

The female flea can consume 15 times her weight in blood during active reproduction and can lay as many as 40 eggs a day. These eggs are very resistant to the effects of insecticides. They hatch into larvae, which then mature and spin cocoons. The immature fleas reside in this pupal stage until the time is right for feeding. This pupal stage is also very resistant to the effects of insecticides, and pupae can last in the environment without feeding for many months. Newly emergent fleas are attracted to animals by the warmth of the animals' bodies, movement and exhaled carbon dioxide. However, when they first emerge from their cocoons, they orient towards light; thus when an animal passes between a flea and the light source, casting a shadow, the flea pounces and starts to feed. If the animal turns out to be a dog or cat, the reproductive cycle continues. If the flea lands on another type of animal, including a person, the flea will bite but will then look for a more appropriate host. An emerging adult flea can survive without feeding for up to 12 months but, once it tastes blood, it can survive off its host for only three to four days.

It was once thought that fleas spend most of their lives in the environment, but we now know that fleas won't willingly jump off a dog unless leaping to another dog or when physically removed by brushing, bathing or other manipulation. Flea eggs, on the other hand, are shiny and smooth, and they roll off the animal and into the environment. The eggs, larvae and pupae then exist in the environment, but once the adult finds a susceptible animal, it's home sweet home until the flea is forced to seek refuge elsewhere.

Since adult fleas live on the animal and immature forms survive in the environment, a successful treatment plan must address all stages of the flea life cycle. There are now several safe and effective flea-control products that can be applied on a monthly

> ### FLEA PREVENTION FOR YOUR DOG
> - Discuss with your veterinarian the safest product to protect your dog, likely in the form of a monthly tablet or a liquid preparation placed on the back of the dog's neck.
> - For dogs suffering from flea-bite dermatitis, a shampoo or topical insecticide treatment is required.
> - Your lawn and property should be sprayed with an insecticide designed to kill fleas and ticks that lurk outdoors.
> - Using a flea comb, check the dog's coat regularly for any signs of parasites.
> - Practice good housekeeping. Vacuum floors, carpets and furniture regularly, especially in the areas that the dog frequents, and wash the dog's bedding weekly.
> - Follow up house-cleaning with carpet shampoos and sprays to rid the house of fleas at all stages of development. Insect growth regulators are the safest option.

basis. These include fipronil, imidacloprid, selamectin and permethrin (found in several formulations). Most of these products have significant flea-killing rates within 24 hours. However, none of them will control the immature forms in the environment. To accomplish this, there are a variety of insect growth regulators that can be sprayed into

THE FLEA'S LIFE CYCLE

What came first, the flea or the egg? This age-old mystery is more difficult to comprehend than the actual cycle of the flea. Fleas usually live only about four months. A female can lay 2,000 eggs in her lifetime.

Photo by Carolina Biological Supply Co.

Egg

After ten days of rolling around your carpet or under your furniture, the eggs hatch into larvae, which feed on various and sundry debris. In days or

Larva

Photo by Carolina Biological Supply Co.

months, depending on the climate, the larvae spin cocoons and develop into the pupal or nymph stage, which quickly develop into fleas.

Pupa

These immature fleas must locate a host within 10 to 14 days or they will die. Only about 1% of the flea population exist as adult fleas, while the other 99% exist as eggs, larvae or pupae.

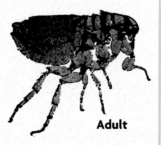

Adult

KILL FLEAS THE NATURAL WAY

If you choose not to go the route of conventional medication, there are some natural ways to ward off fleas:

- Dust your dog with a natural flea powder, composed of such herbal goodies as rosemary, wormwood, pennyroyal, citronella, rue, tobacco powder and eucalyptus.
- Apply diatomaceous earth, the fossilized remains of single-cell algae, to your carpets, furniture and pet's bedding. Even though it's not good for dogs, it's even worse for fleas, which will dry up swiftly and die.
- Brush your dog frequently, give him adequate exercise and let him fast occasionally. All of these activities strengthen the dog's system and make him more resistant to disease and parasites.
- Bathe your dog with a capful of pennyroyal or eucalyptus oil.
- Feed a natural diet, free of additives and preservatives. Add some fresh garlic and brewer's yeast to the dog's morning portion, as these items have flea-repelling properties.

the environment (e.g., pyriprox-yfen, methoprene, fenoxycarb) as well as insect development inhibitors such as lufenuron that can be administered. These compounds have no effect on adult fleas, but they stop imma-ture forms from developing into

adults. In years gone by, we relied heavily on toxic insecticides (such as organophosphates, organochlo-rines and carbamates) to manage the flea problem, but today's options are not only much safer to use on our pets but also safer for the environment.

TICKS

Ticks are members of the spider class (arachnids) and are blood-sucking parasites capable of transmitting a variety of diseases, including Lyme disease, ehrlichiosis, babesiosis and Rocky Mountain spotted fever. It's easy to see ticks on your own skin, but it is more of a challenge when your furry companion is affected. Whenever you happen to be planning a stroll in a tick-infested area (especially forests, grassy or wooded areas or parks) be prepared to do a thorough inspection of your dog afterward to search for ticks. Ticks can be tricky, so make sure you spend time looking in the ears, between the toes and everywhere else where a tick might hide. Ticks need to be attached for 24–72 hours before they transmit most of the diseases that they carry, so you do have a window of opportunity for some preventive intervention.

S. E. M. BY PHOTOTAKE.

A scanning electron micrograph of the head of a female deer tick, *Ixodes dammini*, a parasitic tick that carries Lyme disease.

Female ticks live to eat and breed. They can lay between 4,000 and 5,000 eggs and they die soon after. Males, on the other hand, live only to mate with the females and continue the process as long as they are able. Most ticks live on multiple hosts before parasitizing dogs. The immature forms typically reside on grass and shrubs, waiting for susceptible animals to walk by. The larvae and nymph stages typically feed on wildlife.

If only a few ticks are present on a dog, they can be plucked out, but it is important to remove the entire head and mouthparts,

A TICKING BOMB

There is nothing good about a tick's harpooning his nose into your dog's skin. Among the diseases caused by ticks are Rocky Mountain spotted fever, canine ehrlichiosis, canine babesiosis, canine hepatozoonosis and Lyme disease. If a dog is allergic to the saliva of a female wood tick, he can develop tick paralysis.

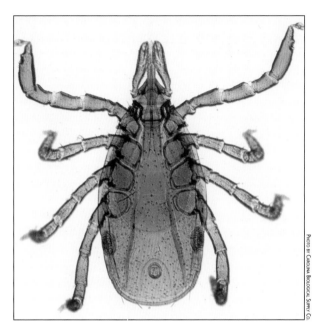

PHOTO BY CAROLINA BIOLOGICAL SUPPLY CO.

Deer tick,
Ixodes dammini.

which may be deeply embedded in the skin. This is best accomplished with forceps designed especially for this purpose; fingers can be used but should be protected with rubber gloves, plastic wrap or at least a paper towel. The tick should be grasped as closely as possible to the animal's skin and should be pulled upward with steady, even pressure. Do not squeeze, crush or puncture the body of the tick or you risk exposure to any disease carried by that tick. Once the ticks have been removed, the sites of attachment should be disinfected. Your hands should then be washed with soap and water to further minimize risk of contagion. The tick should be disposed of in a container of alcohol or household bleach.

Some of the newer flea products, specifically those with fipronil, selamectin and permethrin, have effect against some, but not all, species of tick. Flea collars containing appropriate pesticides (e.g., propoxur, chlorfenvinphos) can aid in tick control. In most areas, such collars should be placed on animals in March, at the beginning of the tick season, and changed regularly. Leaving the collar on when the pesticide level is waning invites the development of resistance. Amitraz collars are also good for tick control, and the active ingredient does not interfere with other flea-control products. The ingredient helps prevent the attachment of ticks to the skin and will cause those ticks already on the skin to detach themselves.

TICK CONTROL
Removal of underbrush and leaf litter and the thinning of trees in areas where tick control is desired are recommended. These actions remove the cover and food sources for small animals that serve as hosts for ticks. With continued mowing of grasses in these areas, the probability of ticks' surviving is further reduced. A variety of insecticide ingredients (e.g., resmethrin, carbaryl, permethrin, chlorpyrifos, dioxathion and allethrin) are registered for tick control around the home.

MITES

Mites are tiny arachnid parasites that parasitize the skin of dogs. Skin diseases caused by mites are referred to as "mange," and there are many different forms seen in dogs. These forms are very different from one another, each one warranting an individual description.

Sarcoptic mange, or scabies, is one of the itchiest conditions that affects dogs. The microscopic *Sarcoptes* mites burrow into the superficial layers of the skin and can drive dogs crazy with itchiness. They are also communicable to people, although they can't complete their reproductive cycle on people. In addition to being tiny, the mites also are often difficult to find when trying to make a diagnosis. Skin scrapings from multiple areas are examined microscopically but, even then, sometimes the mites cannot be found.

Fortunately, scabies is relatively easy to treat, and there are a variety of products that will successfully kill the mites. Since the mites can't live in the environment for very long without feeding, a complete cure is usually possible within four to eight weeks.

Cheyletiellosis is caused by a relatively large mite, which sometimes can be seen even without a microscope. Often referred to as "walking dandruff," this also causes itching, but not usually as profound as with scabies. While *Cheyletiella* mites can survive somewhat longer

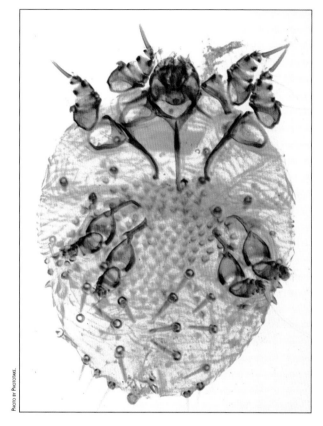

PHOTO BY PHOTOTAKE.

Sarcoptes scabiei, commonly known as the "itch mite."

in the environment than scabies mites, they too are relatively easy to treat, being responsive to not only the medications used to treat scabies but also often to flea-control products.

Otodectes cynotis is the canine ear mite and is one of the more common causes of mange, especially in young dogs in shelters or pet stores. That's because the mites are typically present in large numbers and are quickly spread to nearby animals. The mites rarely do much harm but can be difficult

Micrograph of a dog louse, *Heterodoxus spiniger*. Female lice attach their eggs to the hairs of the dog. As the eggs hatch, the larval lice bite and feed on the blood. Lice can also feed on dead skin and hair. This feeding activity can cause hair loss and skin problems.

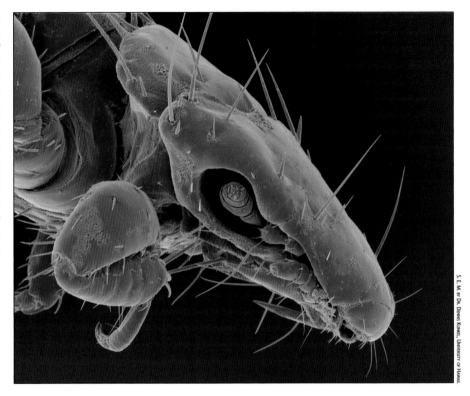

S. E. M. by Dr. Dennis Kunkel, University of Hawaii

to eradicate if the treatment regimen is not comprehensive. While many try to treat the condition with ear drops only, this is the most common cause of treatment failure. Ear drops cause the mites to simply move out of the ears and as far away as possible (usually to the base of the tail) until the insecticide levels in the ears drop to an acceptable level—then it's back to business as usual! The successful treatment of ear mites requires treating all animals in the household with a systemic insecticide, such as selamectin, or a combination of miticidal ear drops combined with whole-body flea-control preparations.

Demodicosis, sometimes referred to as red mange, can be one of the most difficult forms of mange to treat. Part of the problem has to do with the fact that the mites live in the hair follicles and they are relatively well shielded from topical and systemic products. The main issue, however, is that demodectic mange typically results only when there is some underlying process interfering with the dog's immune system.

Since *Demodex* mites are normal residents of the skin of

mammals, including humans, there is usually a mite population explosion only when the immune system fails to keep the number of mites in check. In young animals, the immune deficit may be transient or may reflect an actual inherited immune problem. In older animals, demodicosis is usually seen only when there is another disease hampering the immune system, such as diabetes, cancer, thyroid problems or the use of immune-suppressing drugs. Accordingly, treatment involves not only trying to kill the mange mites but also discerning what is interfering with immune function and correcting it if possible.

Chiggers represent several different species of mite that don't parasitize dogs specifically, but do latch on to passersby and can cause irritation. The problem is most prevalent in wooded areas in the late summer and fall. Treatment is not difficult, as the mites do not complete their life cycle on dogs and are susceptible to a variety of miticidal products.

MOSQUITOES

Mosquitoes have long been known to transmit a variety of diseases to people, as well as just being biting pests during warm weather. They also pose a real risk to pets. Not only do they carry deadly heartworms but

recently there also has been much concern over their involvement with West Nile virus. While we can avoid heartworm with the use of preventive medications, there are no such preventives for West Nile virus. The only method of prevention in endemic areas is active mosquito control. Fortunately, most dogs that have been exposed to the virus only developed flu-like symptoms and, to date, there have not been the large number of reported deaths in canines as seen in some other species.

Illustration of *Demodex folliculoram.*

ILLUSTRATION BY PHOTOTAKE.

MOSQUITO REPELLENT

Low concentrations of DEET (less than 10%), found in many human mosquito repellents, have been safely used in dogs but, in these concentrations, probably give only about two hours of protection. DEET may be safe in these small concentrations, but since it is not licensed for use on dogs, there is no research proving its safety for dogs. Products containing permethrin give the longest-lasting protection, perhaps two to four weeks. As DEET is not licensed for use on dogs, and both DEET and permethrin can be quite toxic to cats, appropriate care should be exercised. Other products, such as those containing oil of citronella, also have some mosquito-repellent activity, but typically have a relatively short duration of action.

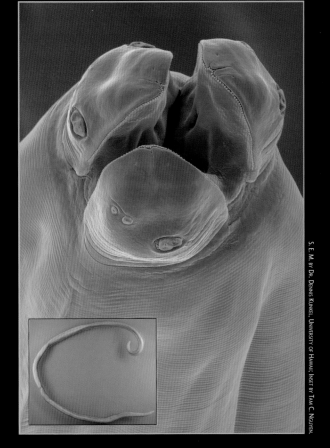

ASCARID DANGERS

The most commonly encountered worms in dogs are roundworms known as ascarids. *Toxascaris leonine* and *Toxocara canis* are the two species that infect dogs. Subsisting in the dog's stomach and intestines, adult roundworms can grow to 7 inches in length and adult females can lay in excess of 200,000 eggs in a single day.

In humans, visceral larval migrans affects people who have ingested eggs of *Toxocara canis*, which frequently contaminates children's sandboxes, beaches and park grounds. The roundworms reside in the human's stomach and intestines, as they would in a dog's, but do not mature. Instead, they find their way to the liver, lungs and skin, or even to the heart or kidneys in severe cases. Deworming puppies is critical in preventing the infection in humans, and young children should never handle nursing pups who have not been dewormed.

The ascarid roundworm *Toxocara canis*, showing the mouth with three lips. INSET: Photomicrograph of the roundworm *Ascaris lumbricoides*.

INTERNAL PARASITES: WORMS

ASCARIDS

Ascarids are intestinal roundworms that rarely cause severe disease in dogs. Nonetheless, they are of major public health significance because they can be transferred to people. Sadly, it is children who are most commonly affected by the parasite, probably from inadvertently ingesting ascarid-contaminated soil. In fact, many yards and children's sandboxes contain appreciable numbers of ascarid eggs. So, while ascarids don't bite dogs or latch onto their intestines to suck blood, they do cause some nasty medical conditions in children and are best eradicated from our furry friends. Because pups can start passing ascarid eggs by three weeks of age, most parasite-control programs begin at two weeks of age and are repeated every two weeks until pups are eight weeks old. It is important to

S. E. M. BY DR. DENNIS KUNKEL, UNIVERSITY OF HAWAII.

realize that bitches can pass ascarids to their pups even if they test negative prior to whelping. Accordingly, bitches are best treated at the same time as the pups.

HOOKWORMS

Unlike ascarids, hookworms do latch onto a dog's intestinal tract and can cause significant loss of blood and protein. Similar to ascarids, hookworms can be transmitted to humans, where they cause a condition known as cutaneous larval migrans. Dogs can become infected either by consuming the infective larvae or by the larvae's penetrating the skin directly. People most often get infected when they are lying on the ground (such as on a beach) and the larvae penetrate the skin. Yes, the larvae can penetrate through a beach blanket. Hookworms are typically susceptible to the same medications used to treat ascarids.

The hookworm *Ancylostoma caninum* infests the intestines of dogs. INSET: Note the row of hooks at the posterior end, used to anchor the worm to the intestinal wall.

WHIPWORMS

Whipworms latch onto the lower aspects of the dog's colon and can cause cramping and diarrhea. Eggs do not start to appear in the dog's feces until about three months after the dog was infected. This worm has a peculiar life cycle, which makes it more difficult to control than ascarids or hookworms. The good thing is that whipworms rarely are transferred to people.

Some of the medications used to treat ascarids and hookworms are also effective against whipworms, but, in general, a separate treatment protocol is needed. Since most of the medications are effective against the adults but not the eggs or larvae, treatment is typically repeated in three weeks, and then often in three

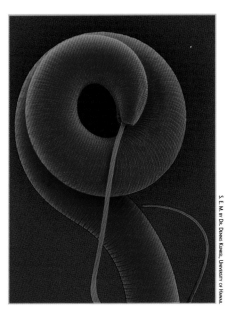

Adult whipworm, *Trichuris* sp., an intestinal parasite.

S. E. M. BY DR. DENNIS KUNKEL, UNIVERSITY OF HAWAII.

WORM-CONTROL GUIDELINES

- Practice sanitary habits with your dog and home.
- Clean up after your dog and don't let him sniff or eat other dogs' droppings.
- Control insects and fleas in the dog's environment. Fleas, lice, cockroaches, beetles, mice and rats can act as hosts for various worms.
- Prevent dogs from eating uncooked meat, raw poultry and dead animals.
- Keep dogs and children from playing in sand and soil.
- Kennel dogs on cement or gravel; avoid dirt runs.
- Administer heartworm preventives regularly.
- Have your vet examine your dog's stools at your annual visits.
- Select a boarding kennel carefully so as to avoid contamination from other dogs or an unsanitary environment.
- Prevent dogs from roaming. Obey local leash laws.

months as well. Unfortunately, since dogs don't develop resistance to whipworms, it is difficult to prevent them from getting reinfected if they visit soil contaminated with whipworm eggs.

TAPEWORMS

There are many different species of tapeworm that affect dogs, but *Dipylidium caninum* is probably the most common and is spread by fleas. Flea larvae feed on organic debris and tapeworm eggs in the environment and, when a dog chews at himself and manages to ingest fleas, he might get a dose of tapeworm at the same time. The tapeworm then develops further in the intestine of the dog.

The tapeworm itself, which is a parasitic flatworm that latches onto the intestinal wall, is composed of numerous segments. When the segments break off into the intestine (as proglottids), they may accumulate around the rectum, like grains of rice. While this tapeworm is disgusting in its behavior, it is not directly communicable to humans (although humans can also get infected by swallowing fleas).

A much more dangerous flatworm is *Echinococcus multilocularis*, which is typically found in foxes, coyotes and wolves. The eggs are passed in the feces and infect rodents, and, when dogs eat the rodents, the dogs can be infected by thousands of adult tapeworms. While the parasites don't cause many problems in dogs, this is considered the most lethal worm infection that people can get. Take appropriate precautions if you live in an area in which these tapeworms are found. Do not use mulch that may contain feces of dogs, cats or wildlife, and discourage your pets from hunting wildlife. Treat these tapeworm infections aggressively in pets, because if humans get infected, approximately half die.

HEARTWORMS

Heartworm disease is caused by the parasite *Dirofilaria immitis* and is seen in dogs around the world. A member of the roundworm group, it is spread between dogs by the bite of an infected mosquito. The mosquito injects infective larvae into the dog's skin with its bite, and these larvae develop under the skin for a period of time before making their way to the heart. There they develop into adults, which grow and create blockages of the heart, lungs and major blood vessels there. They also start producing offspring (microfilariae)

A dog tapeworm proglottid (body segment).

The dog tapeworm *Taenia pisiformis*.

S. E. M. by Dr. Dennis Kunkel, University of Hawaii.

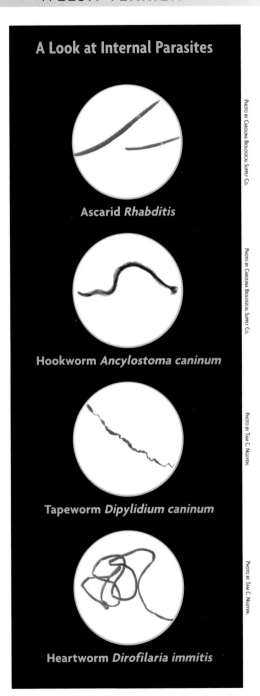

A Look at Internal Parasites

Ascarid *Rhabditis*

Hookworm *Ancylostoma caninum*

Tapeworm *Dipylidium caninum*

Heartworm *Dirofilaria immitis*

PHOTO BY CAROLINA BIOLOGICAL SUPPLY CO.

PHOTO BY CAROLINA BIOLOGICAL SUPPLY CO.

PHOTO BY TAM C NGUYEN

PHOTO BY TAM C NGUYEN

and these microfilariae circulate in the bloodstream, waiting to hitch a ride when the next mosquito bites. Once in the mosquito, the microfilariae develop into infective larvae and the entire process is repeated.

When dogs get infected with heartworm, over time they tend to develop symptoms associated with heart disease, such as coughing, exercise intolerance and potentially many other manifestations. Diagnosis is confirmed by either seeing the microfilariae themselves in blood samples or using immunologic tests (antigen testing) to identify the presence of adult heartworms. Since antigen tests measure the presence of adult heartworms and microfilarial tests measure offspring produced by adults, neither are positive until six to seven months after the initial infection. However, the beginning of damage can occur by fifth-stage larvae as early as three months after infection. Thus it is possible for dogs to be harboring problem-causing larvae for up to three months before either type of test would identify an infection.

The good news is that there are great protocols available for preventing heartworm in dogs. Testing is critical in the process, and it is important to understand the benefits as well as the limitations of such testing. All dogs six months of age or older that have not been on continuous heartworm-preventive medication should be

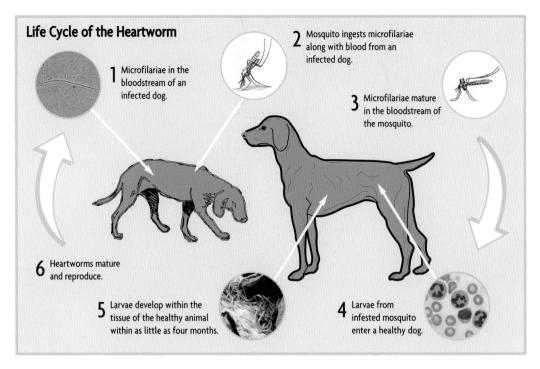

Life Cycle of the Heartworm

1 Microfilariae in the bloodstream of an infected dog.

2 Mosquito ingests microfilariae along with blood from an infected dog.

3 Microfilariae mature in the bloodstream of the mosquito.

4 Larvae from infested mosquito enter a healthy dog.

5 Larvae develop within the tissue of the healthy animal within as little as four months.

6 Heartworms mature and reproduce.

screened with microfilarial or antigen tests. For dogs receiving preventive medication, periodic antigen testing helps assess the effectiveness of the preventives. The American Heartworm Society guidelines suggest that annual retesting may not be necessary when owners have absolutely provided continuous heartworm prevention. Retesting on a two- to three-year interval may be sufficient in these cases. However, your veterinarian will likely have specific guidelines under which heartworm preventives will be prescribed, and many prefer to err on the side of safety and retest annually.

It is indeed fortunate that heartworm is relatively easy to prevent, because treatments can be as life-threatening as the disease itself. Treatment requires a two-step process that kills the adult heartworms first and then the microfilariae. Prevention is obviously preferable; this involves a once-monthly oral or topical treatment. The most common oral preventives include ivermectin (not suitable for some breeds), moxidectin and milbemycin oxime; the once-a-month topical drug selamectin provides heartworm protection in addition to flea, tick and other parasite controls.

THE **ABC**S OF
Emergency Care

Abrasions
Clean wound with running water or 3% hydrogen peroxide. Pat dry with gauze and spray with antibiotic. Do not cover.

Animal Bites
Clean area with soap and saline solution or water. Apply pressure to any bleeding area. Apply antibiotic ointment.

Antifreeze Poisoning
Induce vomiting and take dog to the vet.

Bee Sting
Remove stinger and apply soothing lotion or cold compress; give antihistamine in proper dosage.

Bleeding
Apply pressure directly to wound with gauze or towel for five to ten minutes. If wound does not stop bleeding, wrap wound with gauze and adhesive tape.

Bloat/Gastric Torsion
Immediately take the dog to the vet or emergency clinic; phone from car. No time to waste.

Burns
Chemical: Bathe dog with water and pet shampoo. Rinse in saline solution. Apply antibiotic ointment.

Acid: Rinse with water. Apply one part baking soda, two parts water to affected area.

Alkali: Rinse with water. Apply one part vinegar, four parts water to affected area.

Electrical: Apply antibiotic ointment. Seek veterinary assistance immediately.

Choking
If the dog is on the verge of collapsing, wedge a solid object, such as the handle of a screwdriver, between molars on one side of mouth to keep mouth open. Pull tongue out. Use long-nosed pliers or fingers to remove foreign object. Do not push the object down the dog's throat. For small or medium dogs, hold dog upside down by hind legs and shake firmly to dislodge foreign object.

Chlorine Ingestion
With clean water, rinse the mouth and eyes. Give dog water to drink; contact the vet.

Constipation
Feed dog 2 tablespoons bran flakes with each meal. Encourage drinking water. Mix 1/4 teaspoon mineral oil in dog's food.

Diarrhea
Withhold food for 12 to 24 hours. Feed dog anti-diarrheal with eyedropper. When feeding resumes, feed one part boiled hamburger, one part plain cooked rice, 1/4 to 3/4 cup four times daily.

Dog Bite
Snip away hair around puncture wound; clean with 3% hydrogen peroxide; apply tincture of iodine. If wound appears deep, take the dog to the vet.

Frostbite
Wrap the dog in a heavy blanket. Warm affected area with a warm bath for ten minutes. Red color to skin will return with circulation; if tissues are pale after 20 minutes, contact the vet.

Use a portable, durable container large enough to contain all items

Heat Stroke
Submerge the dog (up to his muzzle) in cold water; if no response within ten minutes, contact the vet.

Hot Spots
Mix 2 packets Domeboro® with 2 cups water. Saturate cloth with mixture and apply to hot spots for 15–30 minutes. Apply antibiotic ointment. Repeat every six to eight hours.

Poisonous Plants
Wash affected area with soap and water. Cleanse with alcohol. For foxtail/grass, apply antibiotic ointment.

Rat Poison Ingestion
Induce vomiting. Keep dog calm, maintain dog's normal body temperature (use blanket or heating pad). Get to the vet for antidote.

Shock
Keep the dog calm and warm; call for veterinary assistance.

Snake Bite
If possible, bandage the area and apply pressure. If the area is not conducive to bandaging, use ice to control bleeding. Get immediate help from the vet.

Tick Removal
Apply flea and tick spray directly on tick. Wait one minute. Using tweezers or wearing plastic gloves, grasp the tick's body firmly. Apply antibiotic ointment.

Vomiting
Restrict dog's water intake; offer a few ice cubes. Withhold food for next meal. Contact vet if vomiting persists longer than 24 hours.

DOG OWNER'S FIRST-AID KIT

❑ **Gauze bandages/swabs**
❑ **Adhesive and non-adhesive bandages**
❑ **Antibiotic powder**
❑ **Antiseptic wash**
❑ **Hydrogen peroxide 3%**
❑ **Antibiotic ointment**
❑ **Lubricating jelly**
❑ **Rectal thermometer**
❑ **Nylon muzzle**
❑ **Scissors and forceps**
❑ **Eyedropper**
❑ **Syringe**
❑ **Anti-bacterial/fungal solution**
❑ **Saline solution**
❑ **Antihistamine**
❑ **Cotton balls**
❑ **Nail clippers**
❑ **Screwdriver/pen knife**
❑ **Flashlight**
❑ **Emergency phone numbers**

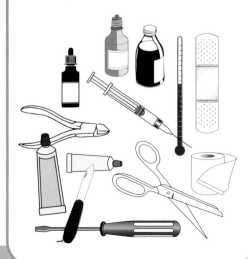

Number-One Killer Disease in Dogs: CANCER

In every age, there is a word associated with a disease or plague that causes humans to shudder. In the 21st century, that word is "cancer." Just as cancer is the leading cause of death in humans, it claims nearly half the lives of dogs that die from a natural disease as well as half the dogs that die over the age of ten years.

Described as a genetic disease, cancer becomes a greater risk as the dog ages. Vets and dog owners have become increasingly aware of the threat of cancer to dogs. Statistics reveal that one dog in every five will develop cancer, the most common of which is skin cancer. Many cancers, including prostate, ovarian and breast cancer, can be avoided by spaying and neutering our dogs by the age of six months.

Early detection of cancer can save or extend a dog's life, so it is absolutely vital for owners to have their dogs examined by a qualified vet or oncologist immediately upon detection of any abnormality. Certain dietary guidelines have also proven to reduce the onset and spread of cancer. Foods based on fish rather than beef, due to the presence of Omega-3 fatty acids, are recommended. Other amino acids such as glutamine have significant benefits for canines, particularly those breeds that show a greater susceptibility to cancer.

Cancer management and treatments promise hope for future generations of canines. Since the disease is genetic, breeders should never breed a dog whose parents, grandparents and any related siblings have developed cancer. It is difficult to know whether to exclude an otherwise healthy dog from a breeding program, as the disease does not manifest itself until the dog's senior years.

RECOGNIZE CANCER WARNING SIGNS

Since early detection can possibly rescue your dog from becoming a cancer statistic, it is essential for owners to recognize the possible signs and seek the assistance of a qualified professional.

- Abnormal bumps or lumps that continue to grow
- Bleeding or discharge from any body cavity
- Persistent stiffness or lameness
- Recurrent sores or sores that do not heal
- Inappetence
- Breathing difficulties
- Weight loss
- Bad breath or odors
- General malaise and fatigue
- Eating and swallowing problems
- Difficulty urinating and defecating

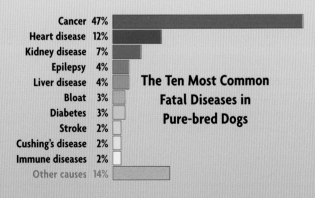

Disease	%
Cancer	47%
Heart disease	12%
Kidney disease	7%
Epilepsy	4%
Liver disease	4%
Bloat	3%
Diabetes	3%
Stroke	2%
Cushing's disease	2%
Immune diseases	2%
Other causes	14%

The Ten Most Common Fatal Diseases in Pure-bred Dogs

WELSH TERRIER

In general, pure-bred dogs are considered to have achieved senior status when they reach 75% of their breed's average lifespan, with lifespan being based on breed size along with breed-specific factors. Fortunately, the Welsh Terrier, like most of his terrier brethren, is a long-lived dog that can live in good health for 12 to 15 years (or even longer) and is considered a senior at around 8 or 9 years of age.

Obviously, the old "seven dog years to one human year" theory is not exact. In puppyhood, a dog's year is actually comparable to more than seven human years, considering the puppy's rapid growth during his first year. Then, in adulthood, the ratio decreases. Small breeds tend to live longer than larger breeds, and terriers, in general, are a hardy lot. Of course, lifespan varies among individual dogs, with many living longer than expected, which we hope is the case!

By the time your dog has reached his senior years, you will know him very well, so the physical and behavioral changes that accompany aging should be noticeable to you. Humans and dogs share the most obvious physical sign of aging: gray hair! Graying often occurs first on the muzzle and face, around the eyes. Other telltale signs are the dog's overall decrease in activity. Your older dog might be more content to nap and rest, and he may not show the same old enthusiasm when it's time to play in the yard or go for a walk. Other physical signs include significant weight loss or gain; more labored movement; skin and coat problems, possibly hair loss; sight and/or hearing problems; changes in toileting habits, perhaps seeming "unhousebroken" at times; tooth decay, bad breath or other mouth problems.

There are behavioral changes that go along with aging, too. There are numerous causes for behavioral changes. Sometimes a dog's apparent confusion results from a physical change like diminished sight or hearing. If his confusion causes him to be afraid, he may act aggressively or defensively. He may sleep more frequently because his daily walks, though shorter now, tire him out. He may begin to experience separation anxiety or, conversely, become less interested in petting and attention.

There also are clinical conditions that cause behavioral changes in older dogs. One such condition is known as cognitive dysfunction (familiarly known as "old-dog" syndrome). It can be frustrating for an owner whose dog is affected with cognitive dysfunction, as it can result in behavioral changes of all types, most seemingly unexplainable. Common changes include the dog's forgetting aspects of the daily routine, such as times to eat, go out for walks, relieve himself and the like. Along the same lines, you may take your dog out at the regular time for a potty trip and he may have no idea why he is there. Sometimes a placid dog will begin to show aggressive or possessive tendencies or, conversely, a hyperactive dog will start to "mellow out."

Disease also can be the cause of behavioral changes in senior dogs. Hormonal problems (Cushing's disease is common in older dogs), diabetes and thyroid disease can cause increased appetite, which can lead to aggression related to food guarding. It's better to be proactive with your senior dog, making more frequent trips to the vet if necessary and having bloodwork done to test for the diseases that can commonly befall older dogs.

The aforementioned changes are discussed to alert owners to what may happen in a dog's senior years. Many hardy dogs remain active and alert well into old age. However, it can be frustrating and heartbreaking for owners to see their beloved dogs change physically and temperamentally. Just know that it's the same Welsh Terrier under there, and that he still loves you and

ADAPTING TO AGE

As dogs age and their once-keen senses begin to deteriorate, they can experience stress and confusion. However, dogs are very adaptable, and most can adjust to deficiencies in their sight and hearing. As these processes often deteriorate gradually, the dog makes adjustments gradually, too. Because dogs become so familiar with the layout of their homes and yards, and with their daily routines, they are able to get around even if they cannot see or hear as well. Help your senior dog by keeping things consistent around the house. Keep up with your regular times for walking and potty trips, and do not relocate his crate or rearrange the furniture. Your dog is a very adaptable creature and can make compensation for his diminished ability, but you want to help him along the way and not make changes that will cause him confusion.

appreciates your care, which he needs now more than ever.

Even if he shows no outward signs of aging, your dog should begin a senior-care program once he reaches the determined age. By providing him with extra attention to his veterinary care at this age, you will be practicing good preventive medicine, ensuring that the rest of your dog's life will be as long, active, happy and healthy as possible. If you do notice indications of aging, such as graying and/or changes in sleeping, eating or toileting habits, this is a sign to set up a senior-care visit with your vet right away to make sure that these changes are not related to any health problems.

To start, senior dogs should visit the vet twice yearly for exams, routine tests and overall evaluations. Many veterinarians have special screening programs especially for senior dogs that can include a thorough physical exam; blood test to determine complete blood count; serum biochemistry test, which screens for liver, kidney and blood problems as well as cancer; urinalysis; and dental exams. With these tests, it can be determined whether your dog has any health problems; the results also establish a baseline for your pet against which future test results can be compared.

In addition to these tests, your vet may suggest additional testing, including an EKG, tests for glau-

coma and other problems of the eye, chest x-rays, screening for tumors, blood pressure test, test for thyroid function and screening for parasites and reassessment of his preventive program. Your vet also will ask you questions about your dog's diet and activity level, what you feed and the amounts that you feed. This information, along with his evaluation of the dog's overall condition, will enable him to suggest proper dietary changes, if needed.

This may seem like quite a work-up for your pet, but veterinarians advise that older dogs need more frequent attention so that any health problems can be detected as early as possible. Serious conditions like kidney disease, heart disease and cancer may not present outward symptoms, or the problem may go undetected if the symptoms are mistaken by owners as just part of the aging process.

Cognitive dysfunction shares much in common with senility and Alzheimer's disease, and dogs are not immune. Dogs can become confused and/or disoriented, lose their house-training, have abnormal sleep-wake cycles and interact differently with their owners. There is good evidence that continued stimulation in the form of games, play, training and exercise can help to maintain cognitive function. There are also medications (such as seligiline) and antioxidant-fortified senior diets that have been shown to be beneficial.

Cancer is also a condition more common in the elderly. Almost all of the cancers seen in people are also seen in pets. If pets are getting regular physical examinations, cancers are often detected early. There are a variety of cancer therapies available today, and many pets continue to live happy lives with appropriate treatment.

Degenerative joint disease, often referred to as arthritis, is another malady common to both elderly dogs and humans. A lifetime of wear and tear on joints and running around at play eventually takes its toll and results in stiffness and difficulty in getting around. As dogs live longer and healthier lives, it is natural that they should eventually feel some of the effects of aging. Once again, if your Welsh has always received regular veterinary care, he should not have been carrying extra pounds all those years and wearing those joints out before their time. If your pet was unfortunate enough to inherit hip dysplasia, osteochondritis dissecans or any of the other developmental orthopedic diseases, battling the onset of degenerative joint disease was probably a long-standing goal. In any case, there are now many effective remedies for managing degenerative joint disease and a number of remarkable surgeries as well.

WEATHER WORRIES
Older pets are less tolerant of extremes in weather, both heat and cold. Your older dog should not spend extended periods in the sun; when outdoors in the warm weather, make sure he does not become overheated. In chilly weather, consider a sweater for your dog when outdoors and limit time spent outside. Whether or not his coat is thinning, he will need provisions to keep him warm when the weather is cold. You may even place his bed by a heating duct in your living room or bedroom.

Aside from the extra veterinary care, there is much you can do at home to keep your older dog in good condition. The dog's diet is an important factor. If your dog's appetite decreases, he will not be getting the nutrients he needs. He also will lose weight, which is unhealthy for a dog at a proper weight. Conversely, an older dog's metabolism is slower and he usually exercises less, but he should not be allowed to become obese. Obesity in an older dog is especially risky, because extra pounds mean extra stress on the body, increasing his vulnerability to heart disease. Additionally, the extra pounds make it harder for the dog to move about. You should discuss age-related feeding changes with your vet.

As for exercise, the senior dog should not be allowed to become a "couch potato" despite his old age. He may not be able to handle the morning run, long walks and vigorous games of fetch, but he still needs to get up and get moving. Keep up with your daily walks, but keep the distances shorter and let your dog set the pace. If he gets to the point where he's not up for walks, let him stroll around the yard. On the other hand, many dogs remain very active in their senior years, so base changes to the exercise program on your own individual dog and what he's capable of. Don't worry, your Welsh Terrier will let you know when it's time to rest.

Keep up with your grooming routine as you always have. Be extra diligent about checking the skin and coat for problems. Older dogs can experience thinning coats as a normal aging process, but they can also lose hair as a result of medical problems. Some thinning is normal, but patches of baldness or the loss of significant amounts of hair is not.

Hopefully, you've been regular with brushing your dog's teeth throughout his life. Healthy teeth directly affect overall good health. We already know that bacteria from gum infections can enter the dog's body through the damaged gums and travel to the organs. At a stage in life when his organs don't function as well as they used to, you don't want anything to put additional strain on them. Clean teeth also contribute to a healthy immune system. Offering the dental-type chews in addition to toothbrushing can help, as they remove plaque and tartar as the dog chews.

Along with the same good care you've given him all of his life, pay a little extra attention to your dog in his senior years and keep up with twice-yearly trips to the vet. The sooner a problem is uncovered, the greater the chances of a full recovery.

RUBDOWN REMEDY

A good remedy for an aching dog is to give him a gentle massage each day, or even a few times a day if possible. This can be especially beneficial before your dog gets out of his bed in the morning. Just as in humans, massage can decrease pain in dogs, whether the dog is arthritic or just afflicted by the stiffness that accompanies old age. Gently massage his joints and limbs, as well as petting him on his entire body. This can help his circulation and flexibility and ease any joint or muscle aches. Massaging your dog has benefits for you, too; in fact, just petting our dogs can cause reduced levels of stress and lower our blood pressure. Massage and petting also help you find any previously undetected lumps, bumps or abnormalities. Often these are not visible and only turn up by being felt.

Ch. Shaireab's On Your Honor, bred and owned by Sharon Abmeyer, is known as "Opie." He won his championship at the Montgomery County show in 2003.

AKC CONFORMATION SHOWING

Is dog showing in your blood? Are you excited by the idea of gaiting your handsome Welsh Terrier around the ring to the thunderous applause of an enthusiastic audience? Are you certain that your beloved Welsh Terrier is flawless? You are not alone! Every loving owner thinks that his dog has no faults, or too few to mention. No matter how many times an owner reads the breed standard, he cannot find any faults in his aristocratic companion dog. If this sounds like you, and if you are considering entering your Welsh Terrier in a dog show, here are some basic questions to ask yourself:

• Did you purchase a "show-quality" puppy from the breeder?
• Is your puppy at least six months of age?
• Does the puppy exhibit correct show type for his breed?
• Does your puppy have any disqualifying faults?
• Is your Welsh Terrier registered with the American Kennel Club?
• How much time do you have to devote to training, grooming, conditioning and exhibiting your dog?
• Do you understand the rules and regulations of a dog show?
• Do you have time to learn how to show your dog properly?
• Do you have the financial resources to invest in showing your dog?
• Will you show the dog yourself or hire a professional handler?
• Do you have a vehicle that can accommodate your weekend trips to the dog shows?

Success in the show ring requires more than a pretty face, a waggy tail and a pocketful of liver. Even though dog shows can be exciting and enjoyable, the sport of conformation makes great demands on the exhibitors and the dogs. Winning exhibitors live for their dogs, devoting time and money to their dogs' presentation, conditioning and training. Very few novices, even those with good dogs, will find themselves in the winners' circle, though it does happen. Don't be disheartened, though. Every exhibitor began as a novice and worked his way up to the Group ring. It's the "working

Here she is world: it's "Rose"! The number-one Welshie for 2003 and 2004, Ch. Tothwood's American Beauty, owned by breeder Arthur Toth, Jr., Dr. Isaac Wood and Marge McClung.

your way up" part that you must keep in mind.

Visiting a dog show as a spectator is a great place to start. Pick up the show catalog to find out what time your breed is being shown, who is judging the breed and in which ring the classes will be held. To start, Welsh Terriers compete against other Welsh Terriers, and the winner is selected as Best of Breed by the judge. This is the procedure for each breed. At a group show, all of the Best of Breed winners go on to compete for Group One in their respective groups. For example, all Best of Breed winners in a given group compete against each other; this is done for all seven groups. Finally, all seven group winners go head to head in the ring for the Best in Show award.

What most spectators don't understand is the basic idea of

conformation. A dog show is often referred as a "conformation" show. This means that the judge should decide how each dog stacks up (conforms) to the breed standard for his given breed: how well does this Welsh Terrier conform to the ideal representative detailed in the standard? Ideally, this is what happens. In reality, however, this ideal often gets slighted as the judge compares Welsh Terrier #1 to Welsh Terrier #2. Again, the ideal is that each dog is judged based on his merits in comparison to his breed standard, not in comparison to the other dogs in the ring. It is easier for judges to compare dogs of the same breed to decide which they think is the better specimen; in the Group and Best in Show ring, however, it is very difficult to compare one breed to another, like apples to oranges. Thus the dog's conformation to the breed standard—not to mention advertising dollars and good handling— is essential to success in conformation shows. The dog described in the standard (the standard for each AKC breed is written and approved by the breed's national parent club and then submitted to the AKC for approval) is the perfect dog of that breed, and breeders keep their eye on the standard when they choose which dogs to breed, hoping to get closer and closer to the ideal with each litter.

Another good first step for the novice is to join a dog club. You will be astonished by the many and different kinds of dog clubs in the country, with about 5,000 clubs holding events every year. Dog clubs may specialize in a single breed, like a local or regional Welsh Terrier club, or in a specific pursuit, such as obedience, tracking or hunting tests. There are all-breed clubs for all dog enthusiasts; they sponsor special training days, seminars on topics like grooming or handling or lectures on breeding or canine genetics. There are also clubs that specialize in certain types of dogs, like terriers, herding dogs, companion dogs, etc.

A parent club is the national organization, sanctioned by the AKC, which promotes and safeguards its breed in the country. The Welsh Terrier Club of America was formed in 1900 and can be contacted on the Internet at http://clubs.akc.org/wtca. The parent club holds an annual national specialty show, usually in a different city each year, in which many of the country's top dogs, handlers and breeders gather to compete. At a specialty show, only members of a single breed are invited to participate. There are also group specialties, in which all members of a group are invited. For more information about dog clubs in your area, contact the AKC at www.akc.org on the Internet or write them at their Raleigh, NC address.

OBEDIENCE TRIALS

Mrs. Helen Whitehouse Walker, a Standard Poodle fancier, can be credited with introducing obedience trials to the United States. In the 1930s, she designed a series of exercises based on those of the Associated Sheep, Police, Army Dog Society of Great Britain. These exercises were intended to evaluate the working relationship between dog and owner. Since those early days of the sport in the US, obedience trials have grown more and more

---

FOR MORE INFORMATION....

For reliable up-to-date information about registration, dog shows and other canine competitions, contact one of the national registries by mail or via the Internet.

American Kennel Club
5580 Centerview Dr., Raleigh, NC 27606-3390
www.akc.org

United Kennel Club
100 E. Kilgore Road, Kalamazoo, MI 49002
www.ukcdogs.com

Canadian Kennel Club
89 Skyway Ave., Suite 100, Etobicoke, Ontario
M9W 6R4 Canada
www.ckc.ca

The Kennel Club
1-5 Clarges St., Piccadilly, London W1Y 8AB, UK
www.the-kennel-club.org.uk

popular, and now more than 2,000 trials each year attract over 100,000 dogs and their owners. Any dog registered with the AKC, regardless of neutering or other disqualifications that would preclude entry in conformation competition, can participate in obedience trials.

There are three levels of difficulty in obedience competition. The first (and easiest) level is the Novice, in which dogs can earn the Companion Dog (CD) title. The intermediate level is the Open level, in which the Companion Dog Excellent (CDX) title is awarded. The advanced level is the Utility level, in which dogs compete for the Utility Dog (UD) title. Classes at each level are further divided into "A" and "B," with "A" for beginners and "B" for those with more experience. In order to win a title at a given level, a dog must earn three "legs." A "leg" is accomplished when a dog scores 170 or higher

LEFT: A tunnel is hardly an obstacle for this athletic Welsh Terrier in an agility trial. RIGHT: Flying high! This agile Welsh clears a jump gracefully with room to spare.

(200 is a perfect score). The scoring system gets a little trickier when you understand that a dog must score more than 50% of the points available for each exercise in order to actually earn the points. Available points for each exercise range between 20 and 40.

Once he's earned the UD title, a dog can go on to win the prestigious title of Utility Dog Excellent (UDX) by winning "legs" in ten shows. Additionally, Utility Dogs who win "legs" in Open B and Utility B earn points toward the lofty title of Obedience Trial Champion (OTCh.). Established in 1977 by the AKC, this title requires a dog to earn 100 points as well as three first places in a combination of Open B and Utility B classes under three different judges. The "brass ring" of obedience competition is the AKC's National Obedience Invitational. This is an exclusive competition for only the cream of the obedience crop. In order to qualify for the invita-

tional, a dog must be ranked in either the top 25 all-breeds in obedience or in the top three for his breed in obedience. The title at stake here is that of National Obedience Champion (NOC).

AGILITY TRIALS

Agility trials became sanctioned by the AKC in August 1994, when the first licensed agility trials were held. Since that time, agility certainly has grown in popularity by leaps and bounds, literally! The AKC allows all registered breeds (including Miscellaneous Class breeds) to participate, providing the dog is 12 months of age or older. Agility is designed so that the handler demonstrates how well the dog can work at his side. The handler directs his dog through, over, under and around an obstacle course that includes jumps, tires, the dog walk, weave poles, pipe tunnels, collapsed tunnels and more. While working his way through the course, the dog must keep one eye and ear on the handler and the rest of his body on the course. The handler runs along with the dog, giving verbal and hand signals to guide the dog through the course.

The first organization to promote agility trials in the US was the United States Dog Agility Association, Inc. (USDAA). Established in 1986, the USDAA sparked the formation of many member clubs around the country.

To participate in USDAA trials, dogs must be at least 18 months of age. The USDAA and AKC both offer titles to winning dogs, although the exercises and requirements of the two organizations differ.

Agility trials are a great way to keep your dog active, and they will keep you running, too! You should join a local agility club to learn more about the sport. These clubs offer sessions in which you can introduce your dog to the various obstacles as well as training classes to prepare him for competition. In no time, your dog will be climbing A-frames, crossing the dog walk and flying over hurdles, all with you right beside

TRACKING

Tracking tests are exciting ways to test your Welsh Terrier's instinctive scenting ability on a competitive level. All dogs have noses, and all breeds are welcome in tracking tests. The first AKC-licensed tracking test took place in 1937 as part of the Utility level at an obedience trial, and thus competitive tracking was officially begun. The first title, Tracking Dog (TD), was offered in 1947, ten years after the first official tracking test. It was not until 1980 that the AKC added the title Tracking Dog Excellent (TDX), which was followed by the title Versatile Surface Tracking (VST) in 1995. Champion Tracker (CT) is awarded to a dog who has earned all three of those titles.

Ch. Rubicon's Sugar Bear, ME, CD, OA, OAJ, CG, CGC, TDI, hunting vermin in a woodpile. Owned by Hiroshi Saito.

he can "work" the quarry by digging, growling or otherwise trying to get the rat, which in fact he cannot touch or harm in any way due to the protective cage.

There are four levels in AKC earthdog trials. The first, Introduction to Quarry, is for beginners and uses a 10-foot tunnel. No title is awarded at this level. The Junior Earthdog (JE) title is awarded at the next level, which uses a 30-foot tunnel with three 90-degree turns. Two qualifying JE runs are required for a

him. Your heart will leap every time your dog jumps through the hoop—and you'll be having just as much (if not more) fun!

EARTHDOG EVENTS

Earthdog tests are held for breeds that were developed to "go to ground" into badger, fox, woodchuck and gopher holes and bring out the quarry. The Welsh and other terriers of like size, or smaller, as well as Dachshunds are eligible to participate in the AKC and AWTA (American Working Terrier Association) trials. These trials test the ability of the dogs to follow the scent underground right up to the quarry. A trench, 9 inches square, is dug and a wooden liner is used to cover the sides and top of the tunnel, which in turn is covered with earth so only the entrance is visible to the dog. The earth floor is rat-scented for the dog to follow up to the caged rat. The dog must then show

NATURAL HUNTS

Completely natural hunting is not only instinctive to the Welsh but also allows the breed to use all its working terrier capabilities to hunt by sight, scent, sound—and digging. In the field, while following scent, Welsh Terriers can often be seen to rise up on their hind legs, or even jump up, to sight prey or to flush it. Going to ground to follow the rabbit, fox, woodchuck or other game is the sequence of the hunt. The terrier follows the prey into the earth and either engages it while the accompanying people can dig it out, kills it or flushes it out of the den—at which point, the chase continues.

Welsh Terrier owners continue to emphasize their dogs' natural instincts by honing them through hunts and trials. Farmers are grateful for these hard working terriers that help rid their fields of destructive vermin.

CANINE GOOD CITIZEN® PROGRAM

Have you ever considered getting your dog "certified"? The AKC's Canine Good Citizen® Program affords your dog just that opportunity. Your dog shows that he is a well-behaved canine citizen, using the basic training and good manners you have taught him, by taking a series of ten tests that illustrate that he can behave properly at home, in a public place and around other dogs. The tests are administered by participating dog clubs, colleges, 4-H clubs, Scouts and other community groups and are open to all pure-bred and mixed-breed dogs. Upon passing the ten tests, the suffix CGC is then applied to your dog's name.

The ten tests are: 1. Accepting a friendly stranger; 2. Sitting politely for petting; 3. Appearance and grooming; 4. Walking on a lead; 5. Walking through a group of people; 6. Sit, down and stay on command; 7. Coming when called; 8. Meeting another dog; 9. Calm reaction to distractions; 10. Separation from owner.

three qualifying runs at this level. The most difficult of the earthdog tests, Master Earthdog (ME), again uses the 30-foot tunnel with three 90-degree turns, with a false entrance, exit and den. The dog is required to enter in the right place and, in this test, honor another working dog. The ME title requires four qualifying runs, and a dog must have earned his SE title to attempt the ME level. The first terrier to earn a Senior Earthdog title was a Welsh.

The AWTA is the precursor of the AKC earthdog events and was started in 1972 by Patricia Lent. The AWTA rules do not extend to the degree of difficulty of those offered by the AKC, but their trials are held nationwide. There is also an emphasis on natural hunting in which many members and their dogs participate. Welsh Terriers have proven their ability in both versions of earthdog trials and in natural hunts.

Here's an accomplished Welsh entering the tunnel at an earthdog trial. Owner, Hiroshi Saito.

dog to earn the title. The next level, Senior Earthdog (SE), uses the same length tunnel and number of turns as in the JE level, but also has a false den and exit and requires the dog to come out of the tunnel when called. To try for the SE title, a dog must have at least his JE; the SE title requires

UNDERSTANDING THE CANINE MINDSET

For starters, you and your dog are on different wavelengths. Your dog is similar to a toddler in that both live in the present tense only. A dog's view of life is based primarily on cause and effect, which is similar to the old saying, "Nothing teaches a youngster to hang on like falling off the swing." If your dog stumbles down a flight of three steps, the next time he hopefully will be more careful, or he may just avoid the steps altogether.

Your Welsh makes connections based on the fact that he lives in the present, so when he is doing something and you interrupt to dispense praise or a correction, a connection, positive or negative, is made. To the dog, that's like one plus one equals two! In the same sense, it's also easy to see that when your timing is off, you will cause an incorrect connection. The one-plus-one way of thinking is why you must never scold a dog for behavior that took place an hour, 15 minutes or even 5 seconds ago. But it is also why, when your timing is perfect, you can teach him to do all kinds of wonderful things—as soon as he has made that essential connection. What helps the process is his desire to please you and to have your approval.

There are behaviors we admire in dogs, such as friendliness and obedience, as well as those behaviors that cause problems to a varying degree. The dog owner who encounters minor behavioral problems is wise to solve them promptly or get professional help. Bad behaviors are not corrected by repeatedly shouting "No" or getting angry with the dog. Only the giving of praise and

THE TOP-DOG TUG

When puppies play tug-of-war, the dominant pup wins. Children also play this kind of game but, for their own safety, must be prevented from ever engaging in this type of play with their dogs. Playing tug-of-war games can result in a dog's developing aggressive behavior. Don't be the cause of such behavior.

approval for good behavior lets your dog understand right from wrong. The longer a bad behavior is allowed to continue, the harder it is to overcome. A responsible breeder is often able to help. Each dog is unique, so try not to compare your dog's behavior with your neighbor's dog or the one you had as a child.

Many things, such as environment and inherited traits, form the basic behavior of a dog, just as in humans. You also must factor into his temperament the purpose for which your dog was originally bred. The major obstacle lies in the dog's inability to explain his behavior to us in a way that we understand. The one thing you should not do is to give up and abandon your dog. Somewhere a misunderstanding has occurred, but, with help and patient understanding on your part, you should be able to work out the majority of bothersome behaviors.

AGGRESSION

"Aggression" is a word that is often misunderstood and is sometimes even used to describe what is actually normal canine behavior. For example, it's normal for puppies to growl when playing tug-of-war. It's puppy talk. There are different forms of dog aggression, but all are degrees of dominance, indicating that the dog, not his master, is (or thinks he is) in control. When the dog

GET A WHIFF OF HIM!
Dogs sniff each others' rears as their way of saying "hi" as well as to find out who the other dog is and how he's doing. That's normal behavior between canines, but it can, annoyingly, extend to people. The command for all unwanted sniffing is "Leave it!" Give the command in a no-nonsense voice and move on.

feels that he (or his control of the situation) is threatened, he will respond. The extent of the aggressive behavior varies with individual dogs. It is not at all pleasant to see bared teeth or to hear your dog growl or snarl, but these are signs of behavior that, if left uncorrected, can become extremely dangerous. A word of warning here: never challenge an aggressive dog. He is unpredictable and therefore unreliable to approach.

Nothing gets a "hello" from strangers on the street quicker than walking a puppy, but people should ask permission before petting your dog so you can tell him to sit in order to receive the admiring pats. If a hand comes down over the dog's head and he shrinks back, ask the person to bring their hand up, underneath the pup's chin. Now you're correcting strangers, too! But if you don't, it could make your dog afraid of strangers, which in turn can lead to fear-biting. Socialization prevents much aggression before it rears its ugly head.

The body language of an aggressive dog about to attack is clear. The dog will have a hard, steady stare. He will try to look as big as possible by standing stiff-legged, pushing out his chest, keeping his ears up and holding his tail up and steady. The hackles on his back will rise so that a ridge of hairs stands up. This posture may include the curled lip, snarl and/or growl, or he may be silent. He looks, and definitely is, very dangerous.

Uncontrolled aggression, sometimes called "irritable aggression," is not something for the pet owner to try to solve. If you cannot solve your dog's dangerous behavior with professional help, and you (quite rightly) do not

> **FEAR BITING**
> The remedy for the fear biter is in the hands of a professional trainer or behaviorist. This is not a behavior that the average pet owner should attempt to correct. However, there are things you should not do. Don't sympathize with him, don't pet him and don't, whatever you do, pick him up—you could be bitten in the process, which is even scarier if you bring him up near your face.

wish to keep a canine time-bomb in your home, you will have some important decisions to make. Aggressive dogs often cannot be rehomed successfully, as they are dangerous and unreliable in their behavior. An aggressive dog should be dealt with only by someone who knows exactly the situation that he is getting into and has the experience, dedication and ideal living environment to attempt rehabilitating the dog, which often is not possible. In these cases, the dog ends up having to be humanely put down. Making a decision about euthanasia is not an easy undertaking for anyone, for any reason, but you cannot pass on to another home a dog that you know could cause harm.

A milder form of aggression is the dog's guarding anything that he perceives to be his—his food dish, his toys, his bed and/or his crate. This can be prevented if you take firm control from the start. The young puppy can and should be taught that his leader will share, but that certain rules apply. Guarding is mild aggression only in the beginning stages, and it will worsen and become dangerous if you let it.

Don't try to snatch anything away from your puppy. Bargain for the item in question so that you can positively reinforce him when he gives it up. Punishment only results in worsening any aggressive behavior.

We've mentioned that many Welsh Terriers extend their guarding impulse toward items they've stolen. The dog figures, "If I have it, it's mine!" (Some ill-behaved kids have similar tendencies.) An angry confrontation will only increase the dog's aggression. (Have you ever watched a child have a tantrum?) Try a simple distraction first, such as tossing a toy or picking up his leash for a walk. If that doesn't work, the best way to handle the situation is with basic obedience. Show the dog a treat, followed by calm, almost slow-motion commands: "Come. Sit. Drop it. Good dog," and then hand over the cheese! That's one example of positive-reinforcement training.

Children can be bitten when they try to retrieve a stolen shoe or toy, so they need to know how to handle the dog or to let an

Properly socialized dogs should show neither fear nor aggression toward other dogs that they meet. This Welsh Terrier and German Shepherd dog are pleased to make each other's acquaintance.

adult do it. They may also be bitten as they run away from a dog, in either fear or play. The dog sees the child's running as reason for pursuit, and even a friendly young puppy will nip at the heels of a runaway. Teach the kids not to run away from a strange dog and when to stop overly exciting play with their own puppy.

SEPARATION ANXIETY

Any behaviorist will tell you that separation anxiety is the most common problem about which pet owners complain. It is also one of the easiest to prevent. Unfortunately, a behaviorist usually is not consulted until the dog is a stressed-out, neurotic mess. At that stage, it is indeed a problem that requires the help of a professional.

Training the puppy to the fact that people in the house come and go is essential in order to avoid this anxiety. Leaving the puppy in his crate or a confined area while family members go in and out, and stay out for longer and longer periods of time, is the basic way to desensitize the pup to the family's frequent departures. If you are at home most of every day, make it a point to go out for at least an hour or two whenever possible.

How you leave is vital to the dog's reaction. Your dog is no fool. He knows the difference between sweats and business suits, jeans and dresses. He sees you pat your pocket to check for your wallet, open your briefcase, check that you have your cell phone or pick up the car keys. He knows from the hurry of the kids in the morning that they're off to school until afternoon. Lipstick? Aftershave lotion? Lunch boxes? Every move you make registers in

his sensory perception and memory. Your puppy knows more about your departures than the FBI. You can't get away with a thing!

Before you got dressed, you checked the dog's water bowl, made sure he has a supply of safe toys and turned the radio on low. You will leave him in what he considers his "safe" area, not with total freedom of the house. If you've invested in pet gates, you can be reasonably sure that he'll remain in the designated area. Don't give him access to a window where he can watch you leave the house. If you're leaving for an hour or two, just put him into his crate with a safe toy.

Now comes the test! You are ready to walk out the door. Do not give your Welsh Terrier a big hug and a fond farewell. Do not drag out a long goodbye. Those are the very things that jump-start separation anxiety. Toss a biscuit into the dog's area, call out "So long, pooch" and close the door. You're gone. The chances are that the dog may bark a couple of times, or maybe whine once or twice, and then settle down to enjoy his biscuit and take a lovely nap, especially if you took him for a nice long walk after breakfast. As he grows up, the barks and whines will stop because it's an old routine, so why should he make the effort?

JEALOUS PETS

In households with more than one pet, one pet must be dominant. This means that one pet gets more attention, sits closest to you, goes out the door first, takes up more room on the bed and in hundreds of other tiny ways exerts his dominance. The pets will occasionally squabble over your unintended partiality, but it's best not to interfere.

When you first brought home the puppy, the come-and-go routine was intermittent and constant. He was put into his crate with a tiny treat. You left (silently) and returned in 3 minutes, then 5, then 10, then 15, then half an hour, until finally you could leave without a problem and be gone for 2 or 3 hours. If, at any time in the future, there's a "separation" problem, refresh his memory by going back to that basic training.

CHASE INSTINCT

Chasing small animals is in the blood of many dogs, perhaps most, and definitely terriers. They think that this is a fun recreational activity (although some are more likely to bring you an undesirable "gift" as a result of the hunt). The good old "Leave it" command works to deter your dog from taking off in pursuit of "prey," but only if taught with the dog on leash for control.

Chasing cars or bikes is dangerous for all parties concerned: dogs, drivers and cyclists. Something about those wheels going around fascinates dogs, but that fascination can end in disastrous results. Corrections for your dog's chasing behavior must be immediate and firm. Tell him "Leave it!" and then give him either a sit or a down command. Get kids on bikes to help saturate your dog with spinning wheels while he politely practices his sits and downs.

Now comes the next most important part—your return. Do not make a big production of coming home. "Hi, poochie" is as grand a greeting as he needs. When you've taken off your hat and coat, tossed your briefcase on the hall table and glanced at the mail, and the dog has settled down from the excitement of seeing you "in person" from his confined area, then go and give him a warm, friendly greeting. A potty trip is needed and a walk would be appreciated, since he's been such a good dog.

CHEWING

All puppies chew. All dogs chew. Terriers are built to chew! This is a fact of life for canines, and sometimes you may think it's what your dog does best! A pup starts chewing when his first set of teeth erupts and continues

"Are you home yet?" A dog left home alone all day will often anxiously await his owner's return.

bone up on the sofa and, in the course of chewing on the bone, takes up a bit of fabric. He continues to chew. Disaster! Now you've learned the lesson: dogs with chew toys have to be either kept off furniture and carpets, carefully supervised or put into their confined areas for chew time.

The wooden legs of furniture are favorite objects for chewing.

Always keep an eye on what your pup puts in his mouth. This pup has chosen a stick over his array of plush toys, which could prove dangerous.

throughout the teething period. Chewing gives the pup relief from itchy gums and incoming teeth and, from that time on, he gets great satisfaction out of this normal, somewhat idle, canine activity. Providing safe chew toys is the best way to direct this behavior in an appropriate manner. Chew toys are available in all sizes, textures and flavors, but you must monitor the wear-and-tear inflicted on your pup's toys to be sure that the ones you've chosen are safe and remain in good condition.

Puppies cannot distinguish between a rawhide toy and a nice leather shoe or wallet. It's up to you to keep your possessions away from the dog and to keep your eye on the dog. There's a form of destruction caused by chewing that is not the dog's fault. Let's say you allow him on the sofa. One day he takes a rawhide

THE MACHO DOG

The Venus/Mars differences are found in dogs, too. Males have distinct behaviors that, while seemingly sex-related, are more closely connected to the role of the male as leader. Marking territory by urinating on it is one means that male dogs use to establish their presence. Doing so merely says, "I've been here." Small dogs often attempt to lift their legs higher on the tree than the previous male. While this is natural behavior outdoors on items like telephone poles, fence posts, fire hydrants and most other upright objects, marking indoors is totally unacceptable. Treat it as you would a house-training accident and clean thoroughly to eradicate the scent. Another behavior often seen in the macho male, mounting is a dominance display. Neutering the dog before six months of age helps to deter this behavior. You can discourage him from mounting by catching the dog as he's about to mount you, stepping quickly aside and saying "Off!"

The first time, tell the dog "Leave it!" (or "No!") and offer him a chew toy as a substitute. But your clever dog may be hiding under the chair and doing some silent destruction, which you may not notice until it's too late. In this case, it's time to try one of the foul-tasting products, made specifically to prevent destructive chewing, that is sprayed on the objects of your dog's chewing attention. These products also work to keep the dog away from plants, trash, etc. It's even a good way to stop the dog from "mouthing" or chewing on your hands or the leg of your pants. (Be sure to wash your hands after the mouthing lesson!) A little spray goes a long way.

DIGGING

Digging, which is seen as a destructive behavior to humans, is actually quite a natural behavior in dogs. If ever a dog was meant to dig, the Welsh Terrier was bred to do the job. However, he is not an offender unless moles or voles live in your yard, in which case the Welsh may actually prove beneficial to your lawn and thus have your forgiveness for any divots incurred in the process.

As earthdogs, Welsh Terriers are not the indiscriminate diggers one might expect. Some individuals will go at it like Welsh miners, but by and large they save their digging prowess purely for going

> ### FOUR ON THE FLOOR
> You must discourage your dog from jumping up to get attention or for any other reason. To do so, turn away from the dog as he attempts to jump up. Do not bump him in the chest, as this can cause injury to the dog. "Four on the floor" requires praise. Once the dog sits on command, prevent him from attempting to jump again by asking him to sit/stay before petting him. Back away if he breaks the sit.

after vermin. Although terriers are most associated with digging, any dog's desire to dig can be irrepressible and most frustrating to his owners.

Domesticated dogs also dig to escape, and that's a lot more dangerous than it is destructive. A dog that digs under the fence is the one that is hit by a car or becomes lost. A good fence to protect a digger should be set at least 12 inches below ground level, and every fence needs to be routinely checked for even the smallest openings that can become possible escape routes.

Catching your dog in the act of digging is the easiest way to stop it, because your dog will make the "one-plus-one" connection, but digging is too often a solitary occupation, something the lonely dog does out of boredom. Catch your young puppy in the act and put a stop to it before you have a yard full of craters. It is more difficult to stop if your dog sees you gardening. If you can dig, why can't he? Because you say so, that's why! Some dogs are excavation experts, and some dogs never dig. However, when it comes to any of these instinctive canine behaviors, never say "never."

BARKING

Here's a big, noisy problem! Telling a dog he must never bark is like telling a child not to speak! Consider how confusing it must be to your dog that you are using your voice (which is your form of barking) to teach him when to bark and when not to! That is precisely the reason not to "bark back" when the dog's barking is annoying you (or your neighbors). Try to understand the scenario from the dog's viewpoint. He barks. You bark. He barks again, you bark again. This "conversation" can go on forever!

You won't believe where your Welsh will stick his nose in search of a tasty reward. Stop a potential thief by removing temptation—don't leave food within your Welsh's reach.

> **STOP, THIEF!**
> The easiest way to prevent a dog from stealing food is to stop this behavior before it starts by never leaving food out where he can reach it. However, if it is too late and your dog has already made a steal, you must stop your furry felon from becoming a repeat offender. Once Sneaky Pete has successfully stolen food, place a bit of food where he can reach it. Place an empty soda can with some pebbles in it on top of the food. Leave the room and watch what happens. As the dog grabs the tasty morsel, the can comes with it. The noise of the tumbling pebble-filled can makes its own correction, and you don't have to say a word.

The first time your adorable little puppy said "Yip" or "Yap," you were ecstatic. His first word! You smiled, you told him how smart he was—and you allowed him to do it. So there's that one-plus-one thing again, because he will understand by your happy reaction that "Mr. Alpha loves it when I talk." Ignore his barking in the beginning, and allow it, but don't encourage barking during play. Instead, use the "put a toy in it" method to tone it down. Add a very soft "Quiet" as you hand off the toy. If the barking continues, stand up straight, fold your arms and turn your back on the dog. If he barks, you won't play, and you

should follow the same rule for all undesirable behavior during play.

Dogs bark in reaction to sounds and sights. Another dog's bark, a person passing by or even just rustling leaves can set off a barker. If someone coming up your driveway or to your door provokes a barking frenzy, use the saturation method to stop it. Have several friends come and go every three or four minutes over as long a period of time as they can spare (it could take a couple of hours). Attach about a foot of rope to the dog's collar and have very small treats handy. Each time a car pulls up or a person approaches, let the dog bark once (grab the rope if you need to physically restrain him), say "Okay, good dog," give him a treat and make him sit. "Okay" is the release command. It lets the dog know that he has alerted you and tells him that you are now in charge. That person leaves and the next arrives, and so on and so on until everyone—especially the dog—is bored and the barking has stopped. Don't forget to thank your friends. Your neighbors, by the way, may be more than willing to assist you in this parlor game.

Excessive barking outdoors is more difficult to keep in check because, when it happens, he is outside and you are probably inside. A few warning barks are fine, but use the same method to tell him when enough is enough.

"What's for lunch?" Has your Welsh taken a place at the head of the table? If so, you need to stand your ground in enforcing the "no-begging" laws.

You will have to stay outside with him for that bit of training.

There is one more kind of vocalizing which is called "idiot barking" (from *idiopathic*, meaning "of unknown cause"). It is usually rhythmic or a timed series of barks. Put a stop to it immediately by calling the dog to come. This form of barking can drive neighbors crazy and commonly occurs when a dog is left outside at night or for long periods of time during the day. He is completely and thoroughly bored! A change of scenery may help, such as relocating him to a room indoors when he is used to being outside. A few new toys or different dog biscuits might be the solution. If he is left alone and no one can get home during the day, a noontime walk with a local dog-sitter would be the perfect solution.

My Welsh Terrier

PUT YOUR PUPPY'S FIRST PICTURE HERE

Dog's Name _____

Date _____ Photographer _____